TEIFI AND CARMARTHENSHIRE CIRCULAR WALKS

by

Paul Williams

First published 2003

© Text and photographs: Paul Williams

Copyright © by Gwasg Carreg Gwalch 2003.
All rights reserved. No part of this publication may be reproduced
or transmitted, in any form or by any means, without permission.

ISBN: 0-86381-838-2

Cover design: Sian Parri/Alan Jones

Published by
Gwasg Carreg Gwalch,
12 Iard yr Orsaf, Llanrwst,
Wales LL26 0EH
☎ 01492 642031   🖹 01492 641502

CONTENTS

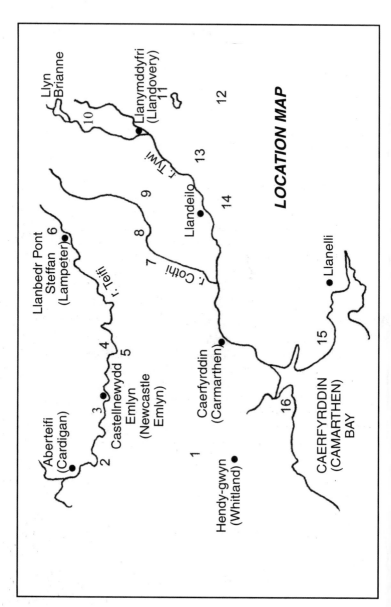

LOCATION MAP

Llyn Brianne

Llanymddyfri (Llandovery) 11

12

10

r. Tywi

13

Llanbedr Pont Steffan (Lampeter) 6

9

Llandeilo

8

14

r. Teifi

7

4

5

Castellnewydd Emlyn (Newcastle Emlyn)

r. Cothi

3

Caerfyrddin (Carmarthen)

Aberteifi (Cardigan)

2

Llanelli

15

1

Hendy-gwyn (Whitland)

16

CAERFYRDDIN (CAMARTHEN) BAY

INTRODUCTION

OUT AND ABOUT

One of the aims of this guide is simplicity. Walks are easy to follow, and clear directions are given. Another aim is variety. Walks have been selected that will highlight both the Teifi river and Sir Gaerfyrddin (Carmarthenshire) county's outstanding landscape beauty and history. The exact location for the start point of each walk is given, and how to get there – however as the walks are circular they may be joined at any convenient point. Relevant bus and train details are included, though not all public services will operate on Sundays, or indeed on all weekdays. Check with Information Centres or bus and train stations for full details. There is adequate parking space at the start of each walk, and precise details are given.

Walks vary in length from 4 miles/6.5 kilometres to 9.75 miles/15.5 kilometres. The routes utilize public footpaths, bridleways and the occasional permissive path. They are well maintained, and clearly signposted and waymarked – a yellow arrow or waymark indicating a public footpath, a blue one a bridleway. Many people are uncertain of how long a walk of, for example 7 miles/11 kilometres would take. As a rough guide an average walker would expect to cover 3 miles/4.75 kilometres an hour over level ground, and on the ascent an hour for every 2000 feet/600 metres. Sketch maps for each walk are provided, the majority based on the 1:25 000 OS (Ordnance Survey) map series. The 1:50 000 scale is catered for by the Landranger series (1.25 inches = 1 mile/2 centimetres = 1 kilometre). The relevant maps for each walk are listed.

The grading system used is largely self-explanatory. Easy walks involve short walks over easy terrain, with little variation in contour. Moderate walks may have one or two short steep sections, with a little more variety in landscape, whilst strenuous walks will involve longer distances, with perhaps greater sections of ascent and descent, and over different types of terrain such as grassland, woodland paths etc. Points of interest are included which are designed to give a quick snapshot of a particular area, what gives a place in landscape or historical terms it's own brand of uniqueness. Under facilities public telephones, toilets, cafés and pubs, shops and youth hostels are listed. Most small towns and many farms will offer B&B – check with Information Centres if you are interested. Also listed under facilities are any additional places of interest in the neighbourhood such as wildlife parks, heritage centres and nature reserves.

Finally a word of warning. Footpaths get muddy, and mountains can be dangerous, particularly in mist. Take care! Ensure you have adequate clothing, and the proper boots or stout shoes, for each walk. Follow the Country Code!

LANDSCAPE AND CULTURE

Carmarthenshire, or to give it it's Welsh name of Sir Gaerfyrddin, is seemingly a county of rivers and rich pasture, but on it's western side the soft improved agricultural grasslands run down to meet the cliffs of Marros and Pentywyn (Pendine), whilst to the south-east the unimproved grasslands and former industrial areas of the county meet sand and estuary. The eastern boundary of Sir Gaerfyrddin is defined by the drowned river valley of the Afon Llwchwr (Loughor) and it's continuation in the Burry Inlet, whilst the centre of Bae Caerfyrddin (Carmarthen Bay) is marked by the Three Rivers system of the Taf, Tywi and Gwendraeth. To the east of the county is the glorious mountain scenery of Mynydd Du (Black Mountain), which is part of the Brecon Beacons National Park.

In size the county comprises some 900 square miles, or 2,230 square kilometres. Much of the north and north-east of the county is underlain by Ordovician and Silurian rocks, with rugged upland areas like Mynydd Malláen. The Old Red Sandstone which gives the Bannau Brycheiniog (Brecon

Beacons) National Park much of it's character extends into Sir Gaerfyrddin under Mynydd Du, and on to the coast around the Three Rivers and on into Sir Benfro (Pembrokeshire). By Pentywyn it is edged by a belt of limestone, and again further to the west by another belt of millstone grit. The great southern Wales coalfield extends into the south-east of the county, Pennant sandstone alternating with the coal, and with a limestone belt at it's north-western edge; adjacent to it on it's southern flank, by Cydweli is a belt of millstone grit. Much of the county's fifty miles/eighty kilometres of coast is low lying blown sand and alluvium, much of it formed only since 1800. Much of the dune system was only formed over the last fifty years. During the medieval and early modern periods Talacharn (Laugharne) and Pentywyn Burrows were absent, estuaries were much wider, and Cefn Sidan's golden sands were absent. There was an island off Llanelli, and from Cydweli to Pen-bre (Pembrey) stretched a great marsh.

The northern boundary of the county is marked by the river Teifi. Rising on the Cambrian Mountains at Teifi pools it runs down through gorges and flat marshy areas to Bae Ceredigion (Cardigan Bay) at Aberteifi (Cardigan). It's origins date back some 380 to 400 million years ago when the plate carrying North America crashed into Europe, with mountain folds forming in a north – south direction. The river began it's development flowing from north to south-west. That other great river of the county, the Tywi, is the longest river in Wales. Also rising on the Cambrian Mountains it flows down into Llyn Brianne, through mountains, gorges and valleys, to Llanymddyfri (Llandovery), Llandeilo and Caerfyrddin, before turning south to Bae Caerfyrddin. Both, together with the river Cothi, are world famous as salmon and sea trout (sewin) rivers.

The county is one of great habitat diversity. Whilst improved grassland has cleared much of the county of it's woodland, much remains. The many river gorges and inaccessible slopes remain home to native species, notably the oak woods of the upper Tywi Valley and the RSPB's (Royal Society for the Protection of Birds) reserve at Dinas, just across the Sir Gaerfyrddin boundary. Notable in the history of Sir Gaerfyrddin was the great Forest of Glyncothi, stretching from the river Cothi to the Teifi. Providing a home to Welsh resistance against English oppression, Edward I was forced to clear the woodland, travelling with specially guarded woodsmen. Nowadays the deciduous trees have largely been replaced by the conifers of the Brechfa forest. The upper Tywi woodlands also played host to later Welsh defenders when it became home to the Cochion Cwm Tywi, the Red Men of Tywi, who had fought with Owain Glyndŵr. Twm Siôn Cati also found the woodland to his liking. It is fair to say that by the end of the Second World War most of the ancient woods had gone, to be replaced by conifer; plantations at Pen-bre on the coast and at Brechfa amongst the first of the new forests.

Water buffalo at Cilgerran Wildlife Centre

Upland areas are largely confined to the north and east of the county, notably Mynydd Malláen, Mynydd Myddfai above the

Wysg (Usk) reservoir, and Mynydd Du – they have all been subject to grazing, resulting in extensive grassland. Mynydd Llanllwni, above the Brechfa forest, does retain heather moorland. Notable amongst the county's standing water bodies is Llyn y Fan Fach, snug and mysterious beneath Mynydd Du, and home to the Lady of the Lake. Like Llyn Llech Owain (at Llyn Llech Owain Country Park, near Llandeilo) it is nutrient poor, unlike other lowland nutrient rich bodies such as Talyllychau (Talley's) lakes, Ffrwd Farm Mire by Pen-bre, Machynys ponds by Llanelli, and Witchett pool between Pentywyn and Talacharn Burrows. In the north the Welsh Wildlife Centre at Cilgerran has both salt-marsh and freshwater marsh, the freshwater being created by the building of the 1885 railway through the saltmarsh. Man made water bodies are rare – there are the upland reservoirs of Wysg, and Llyn Brianne (just over the border by Rhandir-mwyn), and at Cwm Lliedi above Llanelli. There are the disused canals in the Cydweli and Burry Port area, and the ever popular Sandy Water Park by Llanelli. Many new water bodies have been created for the Millennium Coastal Park at Llanelli, including fishing lakes. Close by, at Penclacwydd, is the National Wetland Centre of Wales, with thousands of the world's rarest swans, geese and ducks set within 250 acres of rough pasture, ponds, lakes and saltmarsh. Indeed the Llwchwr estuary which it overlooks has the most extensive area of salt-marsh in Wales, with further areas at the common estuary of the Three Rivers. The Llwchwr estuary and the Burry Inlet are of international significance for it's waterfowl (waders and wildfowl). The area is a Ramsar site (so called after an international convention held on wetlands at Ramsar, Iran, in 1971). Caerfyrddin Bay supports large numbers of common scoter – prior to the *Sea Empress* oil spill in 1996 numbers were as high as 31% of the national population. Major sites for sea-bird colonies are at Telpyn and Gilman Points by Pentywyn. In view of it's threatened wildlife and habitat importance, Caerfyrddin Bay from Dinbych-y-pysgod (Tenby) to Porth

Einion on Gŵyr (Gower), together with it's estuaries, has been designated a Special Area of Conservation (SAC) – full designation is due in 2004.

Man makes his first appearance in Wales at Pontnewydd cave in northern Wales during an interglacial period some 225,000/200,000 years ago, with finds of hand-axes and early Neanderthal teeth – other early hominid remains dating from 500,000 to 400,000 years ago have been found at sites in south-eastern England at Boxgrove and Swanscombe. At Coygan cave near Talacharn tools of Neanderthal type have been dated back to an early glacial period of the last Ice Age some 45,000 years bp (before present). The most spectacular discovery occurred in 1823 at Paviland cave on the nearby Gŵyr peninsula with the finding of the first modern human skeleton in Europe, The Red Lady of Paviland, dating back 26,000 years – by this time Neanderthal man had become extinct. In Sir Gaerfyrddin, at Carreg Cennen's cave, four prehistoric human skeletons have been found buried under a layer of stalagmite. Britain was not fully an island until circa 8,500 years ago, and southern Wales would have existed as marginal land at the edge of Europe, with the Môr Hafren (Bristol Channel) just a river in a wide plain. There would have been little in the way of settlement, but hyenas as well as man would have used the limestone caves strung out alongside the river, and the hyena dens have given up their secret stores of bones of mammoth and woolly rhinoceros, of reindeer and elephant, and of cave bear and cave lion.

With the end of the Ice Age, and the retreat of the ice-sheets some 10,000 years ago the climate improved and the sea levels began to rise. The sub arctic tundra gave way to birch and pine forest, and then progressively to broad-leaf forests. The forests attracted deer, wild pig and cattle, and new tools in bone and antler were developed for hunting, with the rich coastal areas offering attractive fishing grounds, with sea birds and wildfowl part of the menu. Temporary settlements gradually gave way to more permanent sites, and there is evidence of the herding of red deer and of the harvesting of fruit and nuts. Settlements sites were both upland and coastal; there is evidence of possible settlement at Coygan cave at Talacharn. This Mesolithic hunter-gatherer society gradually gave way circa 4,000 BC to the Neolithic era.

With the Neolithic age came a new relationship with the land. The given environment was modified to include domesticated wheat and barley, sheep, cattle and goats. This meant the clearance of the woodland and fixed settlement, a settled home in the natural landscape of the Mesolithic era. It has long been heralded that this Neolithic farming revolution was introduced into Wales, as Britain, by incomers, with the Mesolithic inhabitants forced into the margins, but perhaps it was more of a mixture of the migration of ideas and settlers that forged the new society. Of their day to day settlements, made of wood (only in the Orkneys at the tip of Scotland did the climate require stone) little survives; however the landscape they inhabited is marked by ritual reminders of their presence, the great stone burial chambers. Perhaps with kinship with the land came the need to express that kinship through ritual possession of the landscape and through reminders of their ancestors – the longevity of kin expressed in stone and earth, the symbol of territory and ownership of landscape. There are fine examples of their burial chambers at Ragwen Point by Pentywyn, at Twlc y Filiast (Den of the Greyhound) by Llangynog to the south-west of Caerfyrddin, and a particularly impressive chamber, Gwâl y Filiast (Lair of the Greyhound), just to the north-west of Llanboidy (OS 145 170256).

 It has been argued that the late Neolithic/early Bronze Age eras heralded the development of a new ideology and society associated with the rising and setting sun and moon. There was a

deterioration in climate, with a volcanic explosion in Iceland blotting out the sun, resulting in freezing weather and perpetual rain, along with famine and crop failures. There was a new emphasis on the way of the heavens. Along with the decline in monumental burial chambers – they were replaced by single round burial chambers built on higher and more visible ground than their predecessors, as at Tair Carn Isaf and Uchaf on the western end of Mynydd Du, – went the building of stone circles, henges and stone alignments. These processional alignments could be interpreted as processional journeys from death to the after-life. The larger of the two stone circles of Cerrig y Pigwn (the Peak Stones) above the Wysg reservoir has a recumbent stone to the south-east aligned to the midwinter sunrise. There seems to have been a desertion of settlements and a re-establishment of cleared woodland, though the agricultural system appears to have remained stable. It is believed that the arrival of the Bronze Age (2,000 to 600 BC) was heralded by the immigration of the Beaker people from Europe (so called because of their characteristic decorated pottery drinking vessels), carrying knowledge of copper and bronze, and it's use in weaponry and jewellery, but again as with the Neolithic, it may have been as much a movement of ideas and trade.

The late Bronze Age witnessed a further deterioration in climate and widespread movements of population in Europe. Upland areas were abandoned, and for the first time pressure on farmland resulted in the building of defensive settlements. Strategic sites favoured were coastal headlands and hilltops. This pattern continued with the gradual development of iron working, and as the Iron Age progressed society took on a more aggressive face – the larger forts perhaps exercised some control over the smaller defended settlements and regional grouping formed the basis of future tribal areas. Gilman Point by Pentywyn makes full use of it's coastal setting and natural defensive position, likewise the inland forts of Allt Goch and Goetre by Llanbedr Pont Steffan (Lampeter), but it is at Carn

Goch near Llandeilo that one of the finest examples of the Iron Age fort in Wales survives. One long standing theory has it that it was at the beginning of the Iron Age that the Celts arrived in numbers in Britain, speaking the ancestors of the modern Celtic languages, however there is no evidence to suggest any major influx of people. The so called "Celtic" languages date back to the late Neolithic/early Bronze Age, if not earlier; how and when they arrived in Britain is not known. Society as it developed would have come under the influence of the Celtic mores of Iron Age Europe – however the only real Celts at the time were the continental Gauls.

The Roman period begins with Julius Caesar's landing on the Kent coastline in 55 BC. However Romanisation of the country proper begins with the invasion of Claudius in AD 43 – by AD 78 the conquest of Wales was complete. Existing tribal groupings in the southern of Wales were the Silures of the south-east, with, to the west, the Demetae. The conquest of the Demetae seems to have been quick and efficient, and there is little evidence of Roman settlement west of Caerfyrddin, suggesting that the south-west offered little resistance. However to the east and north were a series of forts defending the main north-south route through western Wales. The Silures, in the mountainous areas of the south, had proved tougher opposition altogether. Julius Frontinus, governor of Britain from AD 74-8, has been credited with planning the roads of Wales, and with the establishment of forts to protect them. There are, near to the Wysg (Usk) reservoir three Roman marching camps, their banks still discernible, and which were thrown up as temporary structures by Roman soldiers during the campaign of subjugation of the Silures. The largest, Arosfa, was capable of housing nearly a full legion. From Caerfyrddin roads ran south to Casllwchwr (Loughor), east to Llanymddyfri, and on passed the marching camps to Y Gaer near Aberhonddu (Brecon), north to the Roman gold mines at Pumpsaint, and on to Llanio and Trawscoed, and northern Wales. The Romans were skilled miners, and gold from Pumpsaint initially probably made it's way on to the Imperial mints of Lyons and Trier.

Alongside the local auxiliary forts grew the civil settlements, or vici. However only Caerfyrddin outlived it's military association to become an urban centre – known as Moridunum (the sea fort), the administrative capital of the Demetae. The original Roman line of defence is still discernible in it's present street pattern and evidence of underfloor heating has been found in one house. The amphitheatre has been partially excavated, and can be visited on the northern side of Priory Street, laid out as a public park. However despite Caerfyrddin's success there is little evidence of Romanisation in the area, other than as a military presence. A few sophisticated buildings have been found, possibly homes of Roman officials, Romanised farms have also been found – there is a possible farm site at Llanboidy, and recent excavations further afield near Tyddewi (St David's) in Sir Benfro (Pembrokeshire) have revealed what may prove to be a substantial Roman villa. There have been the usual finds of pottery, and Roman coins, as at Carreg Cennen and Dinefwr castles. Most of the population lived on in their isolated farms much as before, paying taxes to new masters. By the second century things were stable enough for armed forces to be relocated to the new frontier of Hadrian's Wall; central and northern Wales however remained under military control until the withdrawl of Roman rule in the early fifth century.

With the collapse of Roman rule in the early fifth century the pattern of small scale farming continued, much as it had done during the Iron Age and Roman times, with services and obligations owed by smaller farmers and bondsmen to the 'nobles'. However the removal of a central authority left the land open to raids, first by the Irish – an Irish dynasty was most probably in power in west Wales by the end of the fifth century – and later by the Vikings. The years 400 to 600 were crucial to the formation of Wales as a country, as it was to the Scottish and English nations, and it is the fortunes of the early kingdoms and their rulers that give the period the political flavour of the age. By the mid tenth century it was possible, if only temporarily, for Hywel Dda to have added the kingdom of Deheubarth (Sir Aberteifi (Cardiganshire), Sir Benfro (Pembrokeshire), Sir Gaerfyrddin and Gŵyr) to the northern and eastern kingdoms of Gwynedd and Powys, and to have consolidated the Law of Wales, quite possibly at a meeting held at Hendy-gwyn (Whitland).

Evidence for early medieval settlement has been found at Coygan near Talacharn (a much favoured place throughout early history), but sites are rare. The fifth and sixth centuries was the Age of the Saints, when peregrini, travelling monks from Europe and Ireland, helped consolidate the hold of Christianity in Wales and lay the foundations of the Celtic church. St Teilo, one of the most important of the early Celtic saints, established a monastery at Llandeilo, though all that now remains of it are two Christian crosses. Central to the local community was the llan, so common a feature of Welsh place names, and being an enclosure, often circular (and often making use of an already circular site) for burial. Llan-saint's churchyard (close by Glanyfferi (Ferryside) on the coast) is of this type. Other early Christian evidence derives from the many Christian stones, inscribed with the names of the aristocracy, and marking the site of their graves. Some of the earliest are in Latin and/or ogham – ogham an Irish script of cut notches along the edge of the stone to indicate spelling, an indication of early Irish presence in the area. There is a fine example in Cilgerran's churchyard. Ogham had ceased by 600, later stones being in Latin. More elaborate stones, decorated with linework and fine crosses, may have marked church property. There are memorial stones to two chieftains of Irish origin set in the churchwalls at Llan-saint church. Talacharn's ninth/tenth century disk headed cross has been moved from the churchyard into the church. Llandeilo's two crosses are similarly housed in the church. There is at Scotts Bay near Llansteffan a medieval well in good preservation where a sixth century hermit Anthony used the waters to bless pilgrims on their way to and from Tyddewi (St David's).

The Norman conquest of 1066 was to change the face of Wales. Initially Rhys ap Tewdwr managed to retain his rule over Deheubarth, though acknowledging overlordship to William the Conqueror who crossed his lands in 1081 on a 'pilgrimage' to Tyddewi. However after Rhys' death a series of lordships were established in this south-western corner of the Marches of Wales. Castles were built at Caerfyrddin, Talacharn, Llansteffan and Cydweli, sited not only on strategic high points, but also close to the rivers and sea lanes. Early castles were earth and timber, either ringwork, or motte and bailey, as at Llanbedr Pont Steffan, and subject to constant attack. With consolidation of power and the continuing need for defence, stone was used – Cydweli in the concentric style is one of the finest and most impregnable. The strategic castles of Caerfyrddin and Aberteifi soon came under the power of the Crown. Until the Edwardian conquest of Wales in 1282 Wales outside the Marches – pura Wallia (pure or non Norman Wales) – was allowed to retain it's separate identity. Pre-eminent amongst the Welsh princes of the twelfth century was the Lord Rhys, Rhys ap Gruffydd. He ruled from the Welsh stronghold of Deheubarth at Dinefwr castle, which may be his work. It was a time of stability for Welsh culture; he hosted the first eisteddfod at Aberteifi castle in 1176, with competitors arriving from abroad as well as other parts of Wales. He founded the Premonstratensian abbey at Talyllychau, another at Nanhyfer (Nevern) in Sir Benfro (Pembrokeshire), and rebuilt Aberteifi castle. After his death Llywelyn Fawr held sway in the area. However with his death in 1282, and the end of the Welsh drive for independence, (until the Owain Glyndŵr uprising in the early fifteenth century), the Welsh princes ruled under a watchful English eye. To serve the lords in the castle,

Dinefwr castle

traders and craftsmen settled close by, and in time these communities were granted trade rights and privileges, and later charters confirming borough status. This pattern of urban growth, imitated by the Welsh princes, formed the basis of the urban structure of Wales until the Industrial Revolution. Caerfyrddin was, by the late sixteenth century, the "chiefe citie of the country," with Cydweli and Abertawe (Swansea) among the first rank. Norman society was nothing if not rigid; at the head of it's structure was God, with the King and villein all bound to those above by duty. The expression of that social order was in land, the great estates of the Norman lords, and the obligations of their feudal tenants. The most fertile land was given to their followers, the Welsh were forced to the uplands where they were allowed to keep their customs and law, whilst in the new urban areas settlement was restricted, at least initially, to the non-Welsh, as at Cydweli where Flemings were settled. Of the medieval strip field system there are survivals at the Hugden, Talycharn (Laugharne). Inevitably the Normans found the Celtic church too independent and outdated, and it was quickly remodelled along continental lines. Tyddewi became one of four Welsh dioceses, with outlying churches organised into a parish system; new churches with defensive towers being built on the old llanau, and the dedications to Celtic saints usually being removed and rededicated to Roman ones. Celtic monasticism was also tied to Europe and European orders – a new Cistercian monastery was established at Hendy-gwyn (Whitland) in 1140. Other established religious houses founded included the Knights Hospitallers, with their Welsh commandery at Slebech in Sir Benfro (Pembrokeshire).

By the time of the accession to the English throne in 1485 of Henry VII, born in nearby Penfro (Pembroke) castle, society in the Marches and in Wales as a whole had become more peaceful and orderly. Castles could be modified to become comfortable manor houses, and the Welsh gentry who had leant their support to Harri Tudur as he had taken to the field against Richard III at Bosworth were suitably rewarded. There was greater opportunity for social mobility in society as a whole, and the growth of urban life, the most marked effect of the Norman conquest, continued. The Acts of Union of 1536-43 marked the political merger of Wales with England. The Act of 1536 also fixed the present boundary of Sir Gaerfyrddin, with a minor modification in 1542.

The years from the Acts of Union to 1770 have been 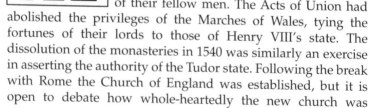 characterised as the age of the gentry, and of the rise of the yeoman farmer. It was they who received the bulk of economic surplus and who exercised control over the destiny of their fellow men. The Acts of Union had abolished the privileges of the Marches of Wales, tying the fortunes of their lords to those of Henry VIII's state. The dissolution of the monasteries in 1540 was similarly an exercise in asserting the authority of the Tudor state. Following the break with Rome the Church of England was established, but it is open to debate how whole-heartedly the new church was

20

adopted. Given the Welsh non-conformist tradition it might be supposed that the mid seventeenth century sects of Puritanism may have had attractions, but again there seems to have been little initial appeal – perhaps it required the urban spark the Industrial Revolution would bring. It was during the Civil War that the castles saw their last moments of glory. However, any which had served the Royalist cause were quickly rendered defenceless by Cromwell after victory. Many were left to fade into obscurity, to find uses in later centuries as Romantic ruins. Dinefwr castle had a summer house added to the top of it's keep in the late seventeenth century for the benefit of it's many visitors.

The years from 1700 to 1850 witnessed an unprecedented two and half times growth in agricultural output in Britain as a whole. Coupled with this, in Wales, as internationally, was a rise in population growth. It has been estimated that in 1500 some 80% of the British population worked on the land, by 1800 this figure had dropped to 30% – the surplus absorbed by the quickening of the Industrial Revolution from the mid eighteenth century onwards. There had been local industry before the revolution; there were textile mills on the Gwendraeth Fach near Cydweli, and the Abertawe area had a long industrial and maritime tradition. By 1820 however the area between Aberafan and Llanelli, part of the southern Wales coalfield, produced 90% of Britain's copper and a large percentage of it's silver, lead and zinc. It was also the centre of the tinplate industry – tinplate was first used to can food in 1825. Once a sleepy village, Llanelli had by 1835 a population of 6000, it's night sky lit by the roaring flames of industry.

In the early years of the nineteenth century the iron industry was pre-eminent in the economy of Wales, and it was on Welsh iron that the trains of the railway era ran – the first to be built in Wales opened in 1839 running from Llanelli to Pontarddulais. The railways replaced the canals and tramroads built by the early industrialists, men like Thomas Kymer who built Wales' first real commercial canal in the Cydweli area from 1766-68. The Kidwelly and Llanelli canal, the most technically advanced in the area, had the ignominy of having rails laid along it's towpath. Alongside the railways went the expansion of harbours and docks at Burry Port and Llanelli. There was a flourishing lead mining industry at Rhandir-mwyn in the north-east of the county, at it's hey-day in the late eighteenth century extraction reached nearly 30,000 tons. From 1850 to 1920 the area around Dre-fach Felindre and the Teifi Valley was the most important region in Wales for the woollen industry. Indeed their reliance on industry rather than on agriculture ensured the development of an urban outlook and culture. Further down river at Cilgerran was one of the most important slate industries, with it's own narrow gauge railway to take away the waste.

Though conditions for many in the new industrial towns were

Dewi Sant Building, University of Wales Llanbedr Pont Steffan

harsh and brutal (as they could be in rural areas) improvements in transport and the growth of urban centres offered increasing opportunities for the growth of popular Welsh politics, religion and culture from the 1870s onwards. For example Llanelli rugby football club was founded in 1875. As early as 1827 Llanbedr Pont Steffan (Lampeter) had opened the doors of the third oldest university in England and Wales, at first with the aim of training young men for the church. The ninetennth century was also the heyday of non-conformism. Chapels, built out of subscriptions raised by local congregations, began to appear in ever increasing numbers in the towns and villages, particularly in the Welsh speaking areas. Indeed as public buildings the chapels are more truly the Welsh vernacular architecture than the English castles. It was also the age of the restoration of the existing Norman and Celtic churches. Since the Reformation there had been little new church building, and existing churches had been either barely maintained or allowed to decay. Old ones were renovated, as at Brechfa, and new ones, with inventive variations on existing styles, were built. The modernisation of society and the economy also meant the gradual end of patterns of trade that had existed for centuries; the smaller coastal trading ports fell into disuse, the herds of cattle of the drovers could now go by rail, and the agricultural fairs were replaced by marts close to urban centres. However some fairs remain; Llanybydder's horse fair is held the last Thursday of each month. The railway age fostered the growth of tourism as an industry, and by the beginning of the twentieth century people were moving into rural areas whose interest in the land was as a source of leisure not agriculture.

Agriculture continued to modernise throughout the twentieth century, with the introduction of subsidies early in the century, and post 1945 new technological innovations and the introduction of chemicals onto the land. The development of local government from the late nineteenth century onwards followed on from the rule of the squirearchy – Sir Gaerfyrddin's county hall is at Caerfyrddin. With the closure of the coalfields and industrial decline came a new initiative to refurbish the Llanelli area, and 2000 saw the opening of the Millennium

Coastal Park. Sir Gaerfyrddin is also fortunate in being the location of the new National Botanic Garden of Wales at Llanarthne near Caerfyrddin – perhaps appropriately enough, as the county is often referred to as the Garden of Wales. Sir Gaerfyrddin and Llanelli have always been strongholds of the Welsh language, and with an eye to the future Llanelli hosted the first National Eisteddfod of the new century.

PLACE NAMES

The study of place-names is a fascinating branch of local history in it's own right, indicating geographical features (which may have vanished), patterns of former land ownership, forgotten buildings or former trades. However the current place-name may be far removed from the original name, particularly where there is an anglicised form of an old Welsh name. Welsh place-names are particularly expressive of geography, and can be highly poetic in combination. Some of the more common names are listed below:

Aber – river mouth, estuary
Afon – river
Ar – on, over
Bach/Fach – little
Ban/Fan(au) – peak, crest, beacon
Banc – bank
Barcud – kite
Bedd – grave
Bedw – birch
Blaen – top
Bre – hill
Bryn – hill
Bwlch – pass
Caer(au) – fort(s)

Caerfyrddin – Merlin's fort (Carmarthen)
Canol – middle, centre
Cantref – hundred (ancient land area)
Capel – chapel
Carn/Garn – cairn
Carreg, pl cerrig – rock, stone
Castell – castle
Cefn – ridge
Cil – nook, source of stream
Clawdd – ditch
Clyn/Clun – meadow
Coch – red
Coed – wood

Coetref/Goetre – woodland, homestead
Cors/Gors – bog, marsh
Craig – rock, cliff
Crib – ridge
Croes – cross
Cromlech(au) – burial mound(s)
Cwm – valley
Cwrw – beer
Cyhoeddus – public
Dan – under
Darren – rocky hillside
Dau – two
Deri – oak tree
Dinas – hill-fort
Dôl – meadow
Du/Ddu – black
Dŵr – water
Eglwys – church
Esgair – ridge
Ffordd – road
Ffrwd – stream, torrent
Ffynnon – fountain, well, spring
Gallt/Allt – hill, cliff, wood
Gelli – grove
Glan – river bank
Glas – blue, green
Gwaun – moor, meadow
Gwyn/Gwen – white
Gwynt – wind
Hafod – summer dwelling
Hen – old
Hendre – winter dwelling

Heol – road
Isaf – lower
Lan – ascent
Llaethdy – dairy
Llan, pl llanau – church, village
Llech – flat stone
Llyn – lake
Llwybr – path, track
Llwyd/lwyd – grey, pale, hoary
Llwyn – grove, bush
Llydan – broad, wide
Maen – rock, stone
Maes – field
Marchog – horseman, rider, knight
Mawr/Fawr – great, big
Meddyg – doctor, physician
Melin – mill
Melyn – yellow
Moel/Foel – bare topped hill
Mwyn – ore, mineral
Mynydd – mountain
Nant – brook, stream
Newydd – new
Ogof – cave
Pant – hollow, valley
Parc – field, park
Pen – head, top
Penlan – top of hill
Pentre – village
Plas – hall
Pont – bridge
Picws – peak

Porth – harbour
Pwll – pool
Rhiw – hill
Rhos – moorland
Rhyd – ford
Sidan – silk
Sir – county, shire
Tafarn – inn
Tir – land, ground, territory
Tomen – mound

Traeth – beach
Tref – town, hamlet
Tri/tair – three
Tŷ – house
Uchaf – upper
Y/Yr – the
Yn – in
Ynys – island
Ysgol – school

A few notes on pronunciation:

c – k (hard)
ch – as in loch
dd – th as in that
f – v
ff – f
g – g (hard)
ll – pronounce l, keep tongue in position at roof of mouth, and hiss!
th – th as in think

There are 7 vowels, a, e, i, o, u, w and y. Pronunciation may be long or short.

w may be as in pool, or pull eg *cwm* (coom) – valley
y may be as in fun, or pin eg *y, yr* (u, ur) – the, *dyffryn* (dufrin) – valley

Many Welsh words change their pronunciation and spelling under certain circumstances, for example the initial consonant of many words may soften: b to f, c to g, m to f, p to b etc. Common examples of mutations are 'bach' (little) to 'fach', 'mawr' (big) to 'fawr', 'porth' (harbour) to 'borth'. Such mutations can make tracing words through a dictionary a little problematic for the uninitiated!

TOURIST INFORMATION CENTRES

Caerfyrddin – Lammas Street	01267 231557
Llandeilo – Car park, Crescent Road	01558 824226
Llanymddyfri – Heritage Centre, Kings Road	01550 720693
Llanelli – North Dock (Summer only)	01554 772020
Castell Newydd Emlyn – Market Hall	01239 711333

FURTHER WALKS/SITES OF INTEREST

Aberglasne
Jacobean garden, with rare Parapet walk. 3 mile west of Llandeilo.

Caerfyrddin Bay Coastal Path.
Links Amroth and the Sir Benfro (Pembrokeshire) Coast Path with the Sir Gaerfyrddin coast. Will extend to the Gŵyr peninsula.

Cilgerran Wildlife Centre
265 acre wildlife reserve close to Aberteifi.

Cwm Lliedi Reservoir.
Situated just to the north-west of Llanelli there is a pleasant circular walk around the reservoir.

Dinefwr Park
Medieval deer and cattle park, with rare White Park cattle, and deer. Several walks possible in grounds, including to Dinefwr castle. Includes the originally seventeenth century Newton House and Victorian Italianate garden. Outskirts of Llandeilo.

Dolau cothi Gold Mines
The only known Roman gold mine in Britain. At Pumpsaint, near Llanbedr Pont Steffan (Lampeter).

Gelli Aur (Golden Grove) Country Park
Includes the magnificent mansion of the Vaughan and Cawdor families, a 20 acre deer park, arboretum with some fine mature trees dating from the mid nineteenth century, and nature trails. South-west of Llandeilo.

Landsker Borderlands Trail

A 60 mile/96 kilometre circular walk taking in south-eastern Sir Benfro and western Sir Gaerfyrddin, with Narberth in Sir Benfro at it's centre.

Llyn Llech Owain Country Park

Lake surrounded by peat bog and forestry. Nature trails. North-east of Cross Hands, south–west of Llandeilo.

Millennium Coastal Park Llanelli and Pen-bre Country Park.

The new park stretches unbroken from the Casllwchwr (Loughor) bridge, boundary of Sir Gaerfyrddin, to Pen-bre Country Park and Cefn Sidan sands. A footpath and cycle-track traverses it's length.

National Botanic Garden of Wales

It's centre-piece is the Great Glasshouse, designed by Norman Foster. At Llanarthne, south-east of Caerfyrddin.

National Wetland Centre of Wales

Thousands of the world's rarest ducks and geese on lakes and salt-marsh adjacent to the Burry Inlet at Penclacwydd, south-east of Llanelli.

Paxton's Tower, Llanarthne

Hard to miss eye-catcher built 1808-1815 for William Paxton, a local landowner.

St Illtyd's Walk

A 64 mile route linking Pen-bre Country Park with Margam Park, east of Abertawe.

Llyn Llech Owain

THE COUNTRY CODE

Enjoy the countryside and respect it's life and work.

Guard against all risk of fire.

Fasten all gates.

Keep your dogs under close control.

Keep to public paths across farmland.

Use gates and stiles to cross fences, hedges and walls.

Leave livestock, crops and machinery alone.

Take your litter home.

Help to keep all water clean.

Protect wildlife, plants and trees.

Take special care on county roads.

Make no unnecessary noise.

Dylan Thomas' Boat House at Laugharne

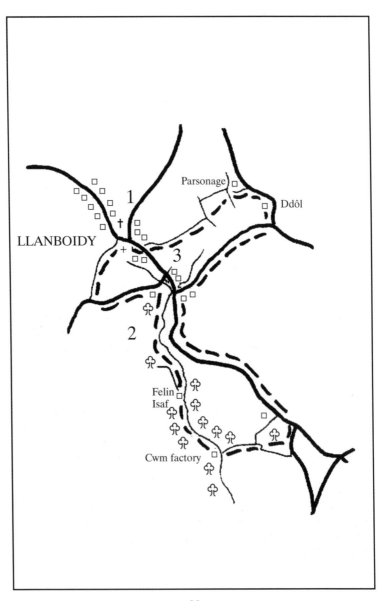

LLANBOIDY

Parsonage

Ddôl

1

3

2

Felin
Isaf

Cwm factory

LLANBOIDY CIRCULAR

OS Maps: 1:50 000 Cardigan Landranger 145, Tenby
              Landranger 158; 1:25 000 Carmarthen & Kidwelly
              Explorer 177.
Start: Car park in Llanboidy.
Access: Llanboidy is 4 miles north of the A40 Whitland
              bypass. Bus 221 Login – Llanboidy – Carmarthen
              Wednesdays and Saturdays only.
Parking: Small car park and picnic site in village.
Grade: Easy – can get muddy and overgrown in places.

POINTS OF INTEREST:

1. 'Barley, wheat, milk in full flood is Llanboidy' runs an old
Welsh poem, and gives the lie of the land; agriculture is the true
key to the community's history. Christian settlement began in
the fifth century with the founding of the first church by St
Brynach, an Irish monk. Brynach had been travelling in the area
and had sought shelter. This however had been refused to him,
and he had sought refuge in a local cowshed. Advised during
the night by an angel to establish a church where he saw a white
sow with piglets, he sighted them close by during the next day.
Thus Llanbeudy, the church of the cowshed. Parts of the present
church date from the thirteenth and fourteenth centuries,
however the chancel and north chapel date from the nineteenth
century, with other additions over the centuries. A new bellcote
was dedicated in 1968, replacing an older one built in 1815
following victory at Waterloo. There are two heraldic shields
from nearby Hendy-gwyn (Whitland) Abbey, set upside-down
in the exterior walls at the back of the church, adjacent to the top
of the left side window. The magnificent Scots pine in the
grounds was planted by Jacobite sympathisers in the late

31

eighteenth century.

With the establishment of the Cistercian Hendy-gwyn Abbey in 1151, the majority of land in the area came under abbey ownership – the name Hendy-gwyn (Whitland) derives from the White Monks, that is to say the white habits worn by the Cistercians. At Cwmfelin Mynach, just to the north-east of Llanboidy, a corn mill once owned by the abbey continued in operation until the early twentieth century. However with the dissolution of the monasteries in the sixteenth century property and land owned by the abbey passed to the Crown, and then on to the first of it's private owners in 1544. By 1565 historical references note the Maes-gwyn estate as the owner of some 4000 acres in the locality. Prosperity grew, helped by Llanboidy's position as one of the most important collecting centres for cattle in the south-west – the riverside path from Hafod Hill pottery to Cwm factory being one of the many drove routes leading out from the village. By the mid nineteenth century the village, following depopulation, became increasingly

Llanboidy church

dependent on the Maes-gwyn estate. W. R. H. Powell, squire and MP for Sir Gaerfyrddin, was responsible for instigating much new building – Piccadilly Square, on the right just passed the church, built in 1871 for local estate workers, the market hall in 1881, Maes-gwyn Arms on the site of an old inn opposite the car park in 1858, and even a racecourse in 1850. In 1880 he opened the Provincial Stores, a farmers' co-operative buying in local produce. The coming of the South Wales Railway from Caerfyrddin to Hwlffordd (Haverfordwest) in 1853, and linking Hendy-gwyn and Sanclêr (St Clears), led to the growth in importance of these two near neighbours, and with the death of Powell in 1889 prosperity declined. There is a fine marble statue of a weeping lady on the Powell vault in the churchyard, sculptured in 1889 following his death. By 1918 most of the estate had been bought by local tenants. Maes-gwyn mansion to the north of the village, is now ruinous.

2. Hafod Hill fort, first recorded some 300 years ago, dates from the late Bronze Age/early Iron Age, 1100 to 1200 BC. Evidence has been found of Roman occupation, suggesting development of the fort into a Romano-Brythonic farm. A Roman road, the *Via Julia*, passed through the parish, and there have been finds of Roman coins. Settlement in the area dates back to Neolithic times; the impressive Gwâl Y Filiast (Lair of the Greyhound) burial chamber (SN 170256) to the north-west dates back to 3000 BC. There are many Bronze Age burial mounds in the area, and cremation urns found at two sites outside the village are on display in the National Museum at Cardiff.

3. No historical references have been found relating to a castle at Llanboidy. However the site indicates a motte and bailey castle, built in wood, and of a type common during the twelfth and thirteenth centuries. Llanboidy falls along the Landsker borderlands – Landsker a possibly Norse term for frontier – the frontier which emerged with the invasions of the Normans into south-west Wales. The Welsh constantly resisted the Norman theft of their lands and the invaders had to consolidate and

33

defend their gains by a series of forts built in a rough line from, and including, among many, Y Garn (Roch), overlooking San Ffraid (St Brides Bay) in Sir Benfro, Llawhaden, Narberth, Talacharn (Laugharne) and Llansteffan on the Sir Gaerfyrddin coast. Important castles were later built, or rebuilt, in stone. Llanboidy's castle may have been Welsh in origin, or an outlier of Norman campaigns – many castles changed ownership several times. By the thirteenth century the Landsker had ceased to have military significance, yet there is still a discernible cultural divide. The settled Norman lands to the south of the frontier in Sir Benfro, with it's 'English' style of settlement, gained itself the title of 'Little England beyond Wales', while to the north are the Celtic heartlands of Welsh landscape settlement and language.

WALK DIRECTIONS   **[-] denotes Point of Interest**

1. Starting from the car park turn left and walk up to the church in the centre of the village **[1]**. Take the road on the left opposite the church and continue downhill, past the social club, to join a green lane leading uphill to a minor road.

2. Turn left and continue downhill. Turn right at Hafod Hill pottery. Pass in front of the buildings to join a woodland path, part of the Landsker Borderlands trail. Above your right are the ruins of Hafod Hill fort **[2]**. Not visible from the path, the site is best seen later on the walk, from the main road into Llanboidy.

3. Where the Landsker Borderlands trail turns sharply to the right continue ahead, passing between the buildings of Felin Isaf. At Cwm factory turn left and cross the footbridge across the river Gronw. The ruins are those of a woollen mill and workers' cottages, last inhabited in the 1930s.

4. Continue uphill on a sunken lane to reach a wire field fence. To the right of the lane, in the corner formed by the fence and the hedge, is a stile. Cross, and keeping the oak tree in the centre of the field to your left, reach a farm gate.

5. Turn left onto a minor road, and again turn left onto the main

road into Llanboidy. Continue on the road to turn right at the next junction. Continue to turn left on the road signposted Cwmfelin Mynach, and passing Ddôl turn left onto the rough track to Parsonage.

6. Just before reaching the gate to Parsonage turn left through a field gate. Turn immediately right, and keeping the hedge on your right aim for the electricity pole ahead – the foot-bridge and stile are just behind it.

7. Cross the stile and go up the rise to the left into the field, and keeping the prominent tree and standing stone to your right, aim for the field gate on the left ahead, adjacent to a hedge.

8. Cross several fields, via stiles and foot-bridges, keeping the hedge on your immediate right, to reach a kissing-gate giving access to the main Llanboidy road and the starting point. The mound from Llanboidy's old castle is clearly visible in the last field before the road [3].

FACILITIES

Post office and shop, pub and public toilets (on the left close to the car park) in Llanboidy. Pemberton's chocolate farm nearby. Hendy-gwyn (Whitland) Abbey, now considerably ruined, is open by appointment only (phone 01994 240867).

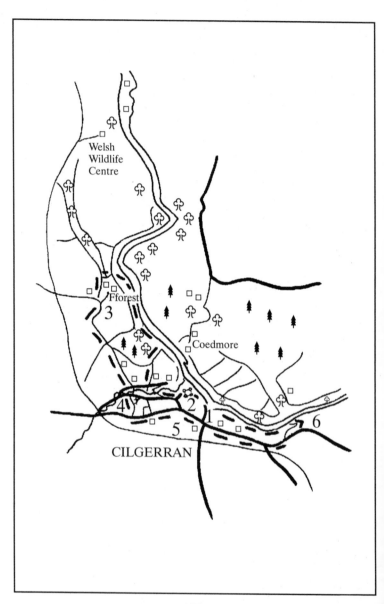

Welsh
Wildlife
Centre

Fforest

3

Coedmore

4

2

1

5

6

CILGERRAN

CILGERRAN CORACLE CENTRE – CILGERRAN CASTLE - FFOREST – CILGERRAN CHURCH AND VILLAGE – CNWCAU – CILGERRAN CORACLE CENTRE

OS Maps:	1:50 000 Cardigan Landranger 145; 1:25 000 North Pembrokeshire Outdoor Leisure 35.
Start:	Cilgerran Coracle Centre.
Access:	Cilgerran is easily reached from the A478 Aberteifi (Cardigan) to Crymych road. Buses 430/431 stop at Cilgerran, en route from Aberteifi to Crymych, Monday to Saturday.
Parking:	Cilgerran Coracle Centre - follow the road down to the river from Cilgerran's main street.
Grade:	Easy - woodland, river and farm paths, road.

POINTS OF INTEREST:

1. Cilgerran gorge, the longest of the Teifi river gorges, is just over 3 miles/5 kilometres long, and owes it's splendid deep isolation to the cutting of the rocks during the Ice Age. The original course lay to the west, along the bed of the present tiny river Piliau. The great Irish Sea glacier is believed to have blocked the original course, leaving the Teifi to cut anew. Downriver, at Aberteifi, the estuary has formed an extensive salt-marsh. The building of the Cardi Bach railway in 1885, from Aberteifi to Hendy-gwyn (Whitland), had the effect of dividing the salt-marsh in two; the result being a freshwater marsh to one side, and a salt-marsh on the other. The railway itself closed in 1963. The Wildlife Trust of South and West Wales has established the Welsh Wildlife Centre here, noting the area as 'without doubt one of the finest wetland reserves in Wales'. It is

well worth the visit for the variety of habitats and wildlife on display – the otter a frequent visitor. Water buffalo are currently being used to help clear vegetation, and open up areas of greater open water.

The river is tidal to just below Cilgerran, and is home to not just the otter but also sea trout (sewin) and salmon, the salmon returning to spawn in the creeks where they were born. The salmon do not always travel alone, as seals follow, and have been seen as far as Cenarth falls, 12.5 miles/20 kilometres from the sea. That other predator, man, has made a living here, fishing from coracles made from local willow, hazel and ash, with skins of hide or calico. The technique is to stretch a net between two coracles, the net being held by hand. At one time a net across the river was connected to a bell at Coedmore, the mansion above the river. Medieval Cilgerran had a salmon weir below the castle, with six traps, and was rated the finest weir in Wales. A later

Cilgerran castle and river Teifi

salmon and sewin weir, below Llechryd's fine stone bridge 2 miles/3 kilometres upstream, was smashed by Rebecca protesters in 1843 in protest at turnpike tolls and at interference with local fishermen's livelihood.

2. In an agreement between William I, a visitor to Tyddewi (St David's) in 1081, and Rhys ap Tewdwr, ruler of Deheubarth (present day Sir Benfro (Pembrokeshire), Sir Gaerfyrddin (Carmarthenshire), Ceredigion and the Gŵyr (Gower)), it was agreed that for £40 a year Rhys could continue to rule southern Wales. However with the death of William in 1087, and Rhys in 1093, it was open day. Earl Roger of Shrewsbury marched as far as Aberteifi, where he built a castle, before moving south where his son established the lordship of Penfro. Penfro castle was eventually given to Gerald of Windsor in 1102, and it was he who crossed the Preseli mountains to establish Cenarth Bychan on what is probably the site of the present castle. Ownership of the castle then passed to alternate attacking Welsh and Normans before a more permanent Norman castle was built by William Marshal the younger in 1223. To William's original drum tower a second was added some years later, which together with strong defensive walls, made it one of the most imposing castles of Wales. Alternatively in disrepair and rebuilt, the castle was by the eighteenth century a Romantic ruin. Boat trips from Aberteifi carried eighteenth and nineteenth century tourists and artists upriver to view the castle, perched as bright as the Romantic imagination on it's rocky crag; among the artists Richard Wilson, Peter de Wint and J. M. W. Turner left their impressions.

3. The woodland along this stretch of the Teifi is typical of the wooded slopes of the gorge, with oaks, ash and wild service trees protected from excessive felling by the steepness of the incline. Fforest farm, a former manor house, was home to Dr Thomas Phaer, physician to Mary 1 and translator of 'Virgil's Aeneid'. He died in 1560.

4. The church is dedicated to St Llawddog, a sixth century

hermit who is believed to have rejected a kingdom - his father was the King of Brysbugah (Usk) – in favour of a life of contemplation. His example gathered followers, and sixth century churches were dedicated to him here at Cilgerran, and at nearby Cenarth. The present church can be traced back to the thirteenth century; the tall Norman tower would have acted as a lookout and extra line of defence for those who could not reach the safety of the castle. However the building had fallen into such a poor state of repair by the mid nineteenth century that in 1855 the whole building, excepting the thirteenth century tower, was completely rebuilt. There is an ogham stone in the ground, inscribed in Latin and ogham, and dedicated to Trenegussus, the son of Macutrenus, who died in the sixth century. Looking much like a worn stone pillar, it is amongst the gravestones to the left of the path leading from the church to the main Cilgerran road. Ogham was a script, invented in Ireland by the fifth century, which uses groups of lines to represent Goidelic, the old Irish tongue. Ogham stones are fairly common in Sir Benfro, and tend to mark the grave of a chieftain. They also provide evidence of strong Irish ties with Sir Benfro and the west in the fifth to seventh centuries.

5. There may have been a village here, clustered around the sixth century church, but written records date the village from the early thirteenth century, with the town growing up around the Norman castle. The town became noted for it's great cattle fairs, with two summer fairs held by 1800. 1800 was a good year for Cilgerran, a total of twenty thousand beasts were sold. Wool was another strong seller, with cargoes taken down to Aberteifi from 1600 onwards for sale, particularly to men from northern Wales, who wove the wool into suitable clothes for sale in Shrewsbury. With the nineteenth century slate quarrying came to the fore, and the town took on the aspect of a quarrymen's village. It is now a popular centre for visitors and fishermen.

NEST, THE HELEN OF WALES

It was Gerald of Windsor who founded the first castle in Cilgerran, Cenarth Bychan, probably in 1108, and probably on the site of the present castle. Gerald was something of a Norman adventurer, who had been given the custody of Penfro castle in 1102 after successful defence of it against the Welsh in 1096. He built a second castle on land at Caeriw (Carew), which he gained as part of the dowry of his new wife Nest, the daughter of Rhys ap Tewdwr, the ruler of the old kingship of Deheubarth (south-west Wales). Nest was well famed for her beauty, and Gerald no doubt felt he was well favoured. Seeking to consolidate his claim to Welsh lands he had chosen his new site with his eyes across the Teifi to Ceredigion. However Gerald was not without enemies, nor Nest without her admirers.

In 1109 Nest's second cousin Owain ap Cadwgan, who also had claims on Ceredigion, paid Nest a visit as a kinsman in her and Gerald's newly fortified castle. Events were later chronicled in the medieval Chronicle of the Princes, and they say that Owain returned later that night with a small retinue of men, surrounded Gerald and Nest's bedchamber, and began to set fire to the buildings, with the intention of burning them alive. Nest advised Gerald to escape by the privy hole adjacent to the chamber, which he, no doubt unhappily, did. Nest then called out that Gerald had escaped, and she and her children – one was Angharad, who was to become the mother of Gerallt Gymro (Gerald of Wales), whose descriptions of Wales and Ireland remain in print – were seized by Owain. She is reputed to have told him that if her children were returned to their father she would stay with Owain. It is also reputedly said that she was perfectly willing to comply with this idea. Owain may also have thought himself fortunate, but Nest was no demur princess, and a series of further amorous adventures were to follow, including for a time, her becoming the mistress of the King, Henry I.

41

Her abduction, her beauty, and her number of lovers and children gained her notoriety, and she gained herself the title of Helen of Wales.

6. The sharp hairpin slope down to the river served as a ramp to carry slate up from the river quarries to the village above. The *Mason's Arms*, at the head of the incline, is still known locally as the *Ramp Inn*. By the nineteenth century the gorge was littered with slate tips and the quays and towpaths where the barges were loaded with slate for transport downriver to Aberteifi. There was even a narrow gauge railway downstream to help trundle away the slate waste, built in response to concerns raised in 1850 about the impact on fishing and the environment from the practice of dumping quarry rubbish in the Teifi. By 1860 five quarries at least were active, with many quarrymen brought down from northern Wales for their expertise, yet by 1891 quarrying had been abandoned. The best slate was exchanged for cargoes of limestone and coal dust (required for mixing with clay to make culm bricks, placed in kilns with the lime to make fertilizer) brought in by ketch from southern Sir Benfro and southern Wales. These were cargoes of sea slate, suitable for billiard tables, roofing and floors, whilst the poorer land slate was sold locally, often for similar purposes. Some of the local slate was used in restoration work on the church, on village buildings, and as tombstones in the chuchyard. In it's heyday the quarry employed some three hundred men, which together with the tinplate works at nearby Llechryd, made the area a hive of industrial enterprise. The remains of the slate industry are still here, re-colonised by nature.

WALK DIRECTIONS   **[-] denotes Point of Interest**
1. Starting from the Coracle Centre **[1]** follow the directions for 'Castle and Village' – there is a path to the left just past the Centre leading up via steps. The Riverside Walk leads to a small

slate stone beach below the castle.

2. Once by the castle entrance [2] turn left and then right onto the road leading to the church.

3. Just past Ger Y Llan - a residential street on the left, there is a footpath right, indicated by a metal sign of a walking man.

4. Follow the footpath downhill to cross a stream, and continue right, in front of houses, turning left uphill to meet a minor road.

5. Turn left onto the minor road, and passing a house and garage, turn right over a stile into a field. Walking man signpost here.

6. Keeping to the right field edge, cross to meet a stile giving access to a pine wood.

7. Follow the path as it turns initially right, and then left, as it follows the course of the wooded Teifi gorge. Good views of the river below.

8. Continue through woodland to the stile at Fforest farm [3]. Ignore the waymark indicating a right turn; instead cross the farm lane, and continuing straight ahead on a permissive path cross another stile giving access to a path leading downhill to meet a farm track.

9. Turn right at the farm track and continue downhill to meet an old quarry on the right. Turn sharp left onto a wooded path by the oak tree – signpost here – the footpath leading straight ahead would take you to the main Aberteifi road, visible through the trees.

10. Continue on the wooded path to meet the farm track leading to Fforest farm. Turn right and follow the track down to a tarmac road.

11. At the tarmac road turn left, and then immediately right. Descend down the stone steps to cross a stream by a concrete foot-bridge, and then ascend to another tarmac road.

12. Turn left and walk uphill to shortly turn right into Cilgerran church [4]. Follow the path through the church grounds, and continue on a path to meet the main road through Cilgerran [5].

13. Turn left and follow the road through the village to the

Mason's Arms in neighbouring Cnwcau. Immediately adjacent to the pub is a footpath, signposted, leading downhill right through woodland, then turning sharply to the left to meet the river [6].
14. Turn left at the river, and follow the track back to the Coracle Centre and the starting point.

FACILITIES

Parking also possible in Cilgerran village. All facilities available in Cilgerran, pub also in Cnwcau. The Welsh Wildlife Centre, just to the north of the village, is highly recommended – canoe trips on the Teifi run from here.

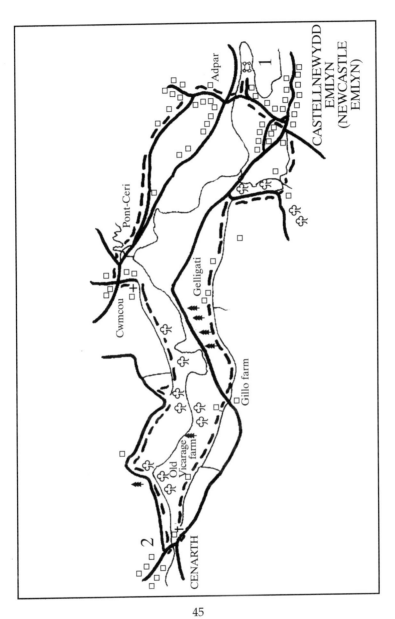

CASTELLNEWYDD EMLYN (NEWCASTLE EMLYN) – ADPAR – PONT-CERI – CWM-COU – PENWENALLT - CENARTH – OLD VICARAGE FARM – GILLO FARM – GELLIGATI – CWM SARAH – CASTELLNEWYDD EMLYN (NEWCASTLE EMLYN)

OS Maps:	1:50 000 Cardigan Landranger 145; 1:25 000 Castell Newydd Emlyn Explorer 185.
Start:	Castell Newydd Emlyn castle. The walk may also be started from Cenarth if preferred.
Access:	Castell Newydd Emlyn and Cenarth are both on the main A484 road from Aberteifi (Cardigan). Buses 460/461 Aberteifi to Caerfyrddin (Carmarthen) both stop at Castell Newydd Emlyn and Cenarth.
Parking:	Free car park by castle. Seasonal car park at Cenarth, or free parking by the river on the Aber-cuch road, if starting from Cenarth.
Grade:	Moderate.

POINTS OF INTEREST:

1. Castell Newydd Emlyn is a busy and bustling market town that was founded outside the castle walls during the fourteenth century. The town's first stone castle probably dates back to circa 1240, when one of the few stone castles to be built in south-west Wales by Welsh rather than Norman hands was constructed by Maredudd ap Rhys. It is almost certainly a replacement for the old motte and bailey castle that lay to the south of Cenarth's bridge. It's prominent position, above a loop of the Teifi, ensured it's strategic value to both Welsh and Norman, and between 1287 and 1289, it changed hands three times during Rhys ap Maredudd's (son of Maredudd ap Rhys)

revolt against the Crown, finally falling to Norman hands with Rhys' death. The gate house, now the castle's most prominent feature, was begun during refurbishment in the early fourteenth century, when the town was founded and it's construction completed by 1349. In July 1403 the castle surrendered, wisely without a fight, to followers of Owain Glyndŵr, however by 1428 the castle was noted as ruinous. A later owner, Sir Rhys ap Thomas, restored it's fortunes circa 1500, and with the addition of windows to the gate house made it more a place of comfort than of defence. It was taken in 1644 by Sir Charles Gerard, and successfully defended for the Royalist cause during the Civil War, only falling to Parliament with the final defeat of Charles I. It was then blown up to destroy any further use of it as a strategic fortress.

There is a fascinating tale relating to the town, and attributed to 1814, in which the last Welsh dragon was slain. Not particularly well behaved, it lived under the castle and made a proper nuisance of itself to the town's people. Finally one Rhys

Castell Newydd Emlyn castle

of Hendre, a veteran of the Napoleonic wars, decided that having faced Napoleon he would face the dragon. Accordingly he put on his red cloak, waded across the Teifi, and shot the dragon. The dying dragon caught Rhys' red cloak, shredded it, and in dying stained the river red and green with it's blood and gore. One explanation of the events notes that when Thomas, Lord Caerew (Carew), took the castle from Owain Glyndŵr's supporters he threw Glyndŵr's red and green flag into the Teifi, and with it Welsh hopes of re-establishing Welsh control in the area instead of the English. Nowadays the town is definitely a Welsh town, the Welsh dragon fiery above the English lion. The town in 1814 was also the site and date of the last duel in Wales, when Thomas Heslop was shot dead by a local solicitor, Gentle John Beynon. Heslop, a West Indian who had been living in Caerfyrddin (it is not known if he was black or white), had accepted Beynon's invitation to join a party for a day's partridge shoot. Following the shoot, arguments broke out over the lack of facilities for shooting, the argument ending up with Heslop challenging Beynon to a duel. Beynon failed to keep the duel's regulation ten paces, and shot Heslop in the back. Convicted of manslaughter he was set free, but was forced into hiding, eventually having to flee to America. In keeping with the Shakespearean fashion of the day for epitaphs Heslop's tombstone reads 'Alas poor Heslop'. Duelling was finally outlawed in 1844.

2. Cenarth is a pretty and popular place, with it's rocks and river, it's waterfalls, and it's long history of leaping salmon and waiting fishermen. As early as the late twelfth century Gerallt Gymro (Gerald of Wales), travelling the country with Archbishop Baldwin to recruit for the third Crusade, noted Cenarth and the rock in the river in his writing. It was believed that St Llawddog, the sixth century founder of Cenarth's original church and monastic settlement, had scooped out a hollow in it to create a '… flourishing fishing station'. Gerallt also commented on the salmon's ability to leap into the hollow

'which is … about as far as the height of the tallest spear'. For centuries Cenarth was famous for it's salmon; remains of medieval fish traps that have been found indicate one method used for catching them, another was by the coracle, either by one man fishing alone, or by two stretching a net between them. In it's heyday in the early 1860s there were over three hundred coracles fishing on the Teifi. The National Coracle Centre in the village gives the history of the craft, both locally and globally. The idea of lashing an animal skin to a framework of branches is a universal idea; here in Wales the earliest used hazel and willow twigs, covered with, preferably, horse hide. Later coracles used flannel, coated with tar, pitch and tallow. Nowadays it is calico proofed with pitch, with an ash board for seating stretched across the frame. These inherently unstable craft are now used in Wales only on the rivers Teifi and Tywi, and require considerable skill from their masters. Unlike the Tywi craft Cenarth coracles have a flattened bow, to assist in navigating the local river. However local their normal use, coracles have been known to take to the high seas; in 1974 one Bernard Thomas paddled his way across the English Channel. The origin of the name appears to derive from the Latin carsula, a little basket – in Welsh this became 'cwrwgl'. The odd salmon still reaches Cenarth, however the seals that once followed them rarely cross the sand bar at Aberteifi.

Gerallt Gymro noted a bridge across the Teifi. However this seems to have fallen into disrepair and disuse over the centuries. The present, attractive bridge is a restored version of William Edwards eighteenth century bridge. The cylindrical holes between the arches were his idea, their aim to reduce the weight of the masonry above – they also prove useful for reducing water pressure during floods. The Coracle Centre now occupies part of what was once the workshop and pig sty of one of the two seventeenth century flour mills that operated here, probably on the site of an older mill that had served Cenarth over the centuries. The mill operated until 1939, reopened in

1954, and occasionally produced until the mid 1980s. It has since been restored. During the nineteenth century Cenarth was an important link of the Caerfyrddin to Aberteifi coach, and the *Three Horses Inn* was purpose built in the early part of that century as a coaching inn and horse change station – the present *Three Horseshoes* was built on the site of the coaching inn later in the nineteenth century. Opposite the inn, what was once the old vicarage and later village school, became a forge for the coach horses. Cenarth was also on the main drove-road for pigs and cattle on the hoof from Aberteifi to Castell Newydd Emlyn, and would no doubt have provided additional work for the smithy. Cattle bound for long journeys were shod; often old pony shoes were used, cut in half, and nailed each side of the hoof. Each drover on longer routes was usually mounted, with a hundred bullocks or so under his charge, and often with a corgi to act as heeler. Adapting to changing times Cenarth's smithy remained in business until 1953. The walk route to Castell Newydd Emlyn utilises part of the old drove road.

Next to the *Three Horseshoes* is Cenarth's oldest building, the appropriately named Old Brewhouse. Although renovated it dates back to medieval times, and has a fine thatched roof. Alehouses like these were often referred to as church alehouses, as church-goers from the outlying farms were offered refreshments, and the profits went to the upkeep of the church. The present church, on the site of St Llawddog's older settlement, dates from the nineteenth century, and has a thirteenth century font decorated with four masks – it was removed from a neighbouring Sir Gaerfyrddin church in the nineteenth century. Like many of its kind it may also have seen service as a pig-trough at a local farm during it's long history. In the churchyard is the Gellidywyll Stone, a three sided stone with an inscription to 'Curcagnus, son of Andagellus', tying it in with another near Maenclochog, ten miles away, to 'Andagellus, son of Caveti'. Before being brought to the churchyard for safe keeping in 1896 it is believed to have been taken to Gellidywyll, a local mansion due south of Cenarth, from either a local field close by the church, or from Maenclochog itself, to act as a memorial to a favourite horse.

WALK DIRECTIONS   **[-] denotes Point of Interest**
1. Starting from the castle **[1]** car park walk back up the road passed the Tourist Information Centre, and turn right onto the main road. Cross the bridge into Adpar (site of the first printing press in Wales, set up in 1718), and continue uphill ignoring the turning left signposted B4333 Aber-porth.
2. After a short distance turn left onto a minor road – there is a letter-box set in the wall on a building on the left. Follow this road to reach Pont-Ceri. Continue ahead on the minor road through houses, cross the bridge, and turn right onto the main road.
3. Continue the short distance to Cwm-cou. At the cross-roads turn sharply to the left on the No Through road marked Lon Drewen. Continue downhill, passed a smart chapel on the right, to reach a path.
4. Continue on the path, and where it divides take the path on the right leading uphill. Continue on the path to reach a kissing -gate giving access to a field. Cross the field to another kissing-gate in the hedge opposite, just to the right of the farm gate on the bottom left.
5. Turn left onto the minor road and follow this until, just passed the turn to Alltgudd Fawr, turn left over a stile and continue along this river path to reach Cenarth **[2]**.
6. Cross the bridge and follow the left fork. Just passed the *Three Horseshoes Inn* enter the church and follow the path through the grounds. Cross the stile and turn left onto the road. As the road bends right leave right on a marked bridleway just before a house entrance.
7. Follow the path to reach a field. Cross the field, keeping to the right edge, to reach a green lane. Continue to reach the road to Old Vicarage farm. Follow this to reach some pens where the

road bends right. Go straight ahead on the green lane and follow this until it joins the road leading right to the main A484.

8. Cross the road and, passing a clipped hedge Humpty Dumpty at the property on the right, continue to reach a green lane by Gillo farm. Follow this well defined lane to reach a metalled track at Gelligati. Continue ahead to reach a minor road.

9. Turn right and continue uphill, until just where the road bends right, descend left by a telegraph pole. Follow the road, via ford/foot-bridge, as it bends left and uphill to reach another minor road.

10. Turn left, and then right, and crossing the road turn left at Porth Street. Follow this to reach the main road through Castell Newydd Emlyn. Turn left again, and follow the road until it turns right for the castle and the starting point.

FACILITIES

Most available in Castell Newydd Emlyn and Cenarth. Tourist Information Centre in Castell Newydd Emlyn, sited in Cawdor hall, with it's clock-tower and covered market. Livestock market on Fridays. National Coracle Centre and renovated flour mill in Cenarth (open Easter to end October, Sun-Fri); small museum dedicated to the former smithy in the craft and gift shop opposite the *Three Horseshoes Inn.*

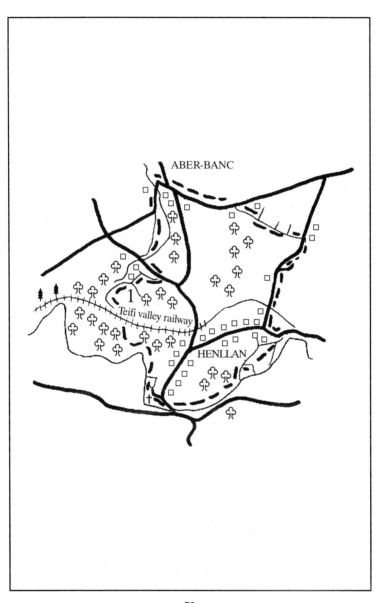

HENLLAN AND TEIFI VALLEY
RAILWAY CIRCULAR

OS Maps:	1:50 000 Cardigan Landranger 145; 1:25 000 Castell Newydd Emlyn (Newcastle Emlyn) Explorer 185.
Start:	Bridge across the river Teifi, giving access to Henllan.
Access:	Henllan is on the B4334, and can be reached both from the A484 Castell Newydd Emlyn to Llangeler, and the A475 Castell Newydd Emlyn to Llanbedr Pont Steffan (Lampeter) main roads. Bus service 460/461 Aberteifi (Cardigan) to Caerfyrddin (Carmarthen) stops at Henllan.
Parking:	On the side-road, close to the starting point.
Grade:	Easy.

POINTS OF INTEREST:

1. Henllan during the growth of the railways came to prominence as a station and passing loop on the Llandysul to Castell Newydd Emlyn seven mile branch line, off the main Caerfyrddin to Aberystwyth line. Plans for a broad gauge line from Caerfyrddin to Aberteifi were first mooted in 1853, the line becoming intention in 1854 with the Carmarthen (Caerfyrddin) and Cardigan (Aberteifi) Railway Act. The Caerfyrddin and Aberteifi Railway started as an ambitious project, with plans for a deep water port in Aberteifi, but development proceeded by fits and starts. Construction finally began in 1857, and Llandysul was reached in 1864. Just when long laid plans to extend the line to Castell Newydd Emlyn were granted to the Caerfyrddin and Aberteifi Railway it was absorbed, in 1881, by the Great Western Railway (GWR). The idea of any extension to

Aberteifi had long been abandoned by all parties, as had Aberteifi's future as a port. Indeed by 1886 Aberteifi could be reached by rail from Hendy-gwyn (Whitland) – via the Cardi Bach railway. Work began on the Castell Newydd Emlyn extension in 1885; however the GWR was in no hurry to complete, and the line did not open until ten years later in 1895.

For the residents of Castell Newydd Emlyn and environs it was well worth the wait. The inaugural train, on July 1, was decorated with flowers and flags, and the *New Market House* played host to two thousand people for afternoon tea. The *Emlyn Arms* hotel hosted a banquet in the evening. The local *Cardigan and Teifiside Advertiser* heralded the piercing sound of the whistle. As was to be expected it was primarily a rural service, serving local towns, and villages like Henllan and Aber-banc. The line transported the products of the woollen industry, coal, cattle and milk churns from the local farms. It's passengers were children on their way to school, and farmers to local markets, with the occasional long distance traveller. The line

River Teifi by Henllan

stayed open for passengers until 1952, with the final closure to freight in 1973.

The track bed was bought by a local society in 1981, and with the taming of the undergrowth and successful drainage of the track, lines were re-laid. The Teifi Valley Railway – one of Wales' great little railways – opened to passengers in 1986, with a further extension opening in 1990. The line is now some two miles long, with both steam and diesel locomotives in action along it's narrow gauge line. The southern section of the old Caerfyrddin and Aberteifi Railway has also been partly restored, the Gwili Railway operating from *Bronwydd Arms*, along the Gwili Valley to Dan-y-coed.

WALK DIRECTIONS [-] denotes Point of Interest

1. Starting from the Henllan side of the bridge across the river Teifi, go through the gate fronting the river path. Continue on the path, and where offered a choice of left and right stay on the right-hand path. The path turns inland alongside a stream to reach a foot-bridge. Cross and follow a faint grass track to reach a waymarked kissing-gate in the hedge to the left.

2. Enter the field and aim for the top right corner to reach a gate and stone steps. Cross and turn left up the steps to reach a minor road. Turn left, and then right at a T junction. Continue up the road to turn left at a waymarked sign, opposite a house to the right.

3. Cross a stile to enter a field, and keeping to the left edge continue to join a green lane leading directly ahead. When the path enters a field continue ahead to leave on the right across a double stile three quarters of the way along the right-hand hedge. There are good views left of the wind turbines on Moelfre hill to the south-west. Continue along the left edge of the new field to cross stiles leading to the main A475.

4. Turn left and continue through the attractive village of Aber-banc. Where the road turns sharply to the right bear left over a stile and bear right along the top of a bank, keeping the hedge

to your right. Where a hedge is met directly ahead continue to the bottom left of the narrow field to cross a stile and join a path leading to the minor road to Henllan.

5. Turn left onto the minor road and cross the bridge - there is an oval plaque in the bridge wall on the right noting it's construction in 1840. Shortly after the bridge leave sharp right and continue on the track to Cae Cadw. Just before the property gate there is a stile on the left. Cross and keeping to the right edge, reach and cross another stile, to then shortly cross by another stile on the right to join a green lane leading away from Cae Cadw.

6. Continue on the green lane/track, and follow it as it bears left and then right to reach a gate giving access to a bridge of the Teifi Valley Railway – this is the Forest Halt [1]. Hop over the gate – it is welded in place – and continue under the bridge, through the gate ahead (this one opens), and stay on the path to meet a stile and gate. Cross and bear sharp left.

7. Continue on the path through the woods to emerge into a field. Bear down right to a stile in the right-hand corner, adjacent to the treatment works. Continue ahead to gate and stile and track which will take you back to the minor Henllan road, passing Dewi Sant church on the right on the way. Turn right at the minor road to gain the starting point.

FACILITIES

The Teifi Valley Railway, open February half term, and Easter through to October, has tearooms, shops and toilets, with crazy golf and quoits – and of course steam trains! Steam trains operate on certain days only, currently Sundays, Mondays and Tuesdays. Check on phone 01559 371077 if you are keen.

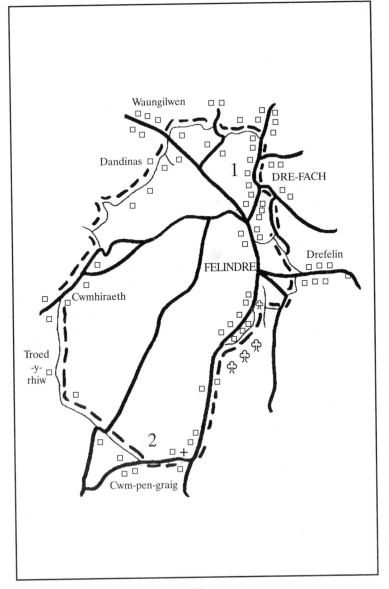

Waungilwen

Dandinas

1

DRE-FACH

Drefelin

FELINDRE

Cwmhiraeth

Troed
-y-
rhiw

2

Cwm-pen-graig

DREFACH – DANDINAS – CWMHIRAETH – TROED-Y-RHIW – CWMPENGRAIG – DREFELIN – DREFACH

OS Maps: 1:50 000 Cardigan Landranger 145; 1:25 000
             Newcastle Emlyn/Castell Newydd Emlyn
             Explorer 185.
Start: Adjacent to the Museum of the Welsh Woollen
             Industry in Dre-fach Felindre.
Access: Dre-fach Felindre is to the south of the A484
             Castell Newydd Emlyn (Newcastle Emlyn) main
             road. Bus 460/461 Aberteifi (Cardigan) – Castell
             Newydd Emlyn – Dre-fach – Caerfyrddin
             (Carmarthen).
Parking: Possible at museum if visiting, or on the main road
             close by.
Grade: Moderate.

POINTS OF INTEREST:

1. Historically the woollen industry has always been one of the most important of the industries of Wales. Whether working from the home or the factory the weavers and spinners, the dyers, fullers and stocking knitters were part of the fabric of country life. At various times in history one area or another in Wales predominated in coming to the fore as a textile manufacturing region – Welsh cloth and flannel seemingly always being favoured for export, and valued particularly for it's especial softness. From 1850 to 1920 the Teifi Valley was Wales' most important manufacturing region; the most important centres at Henllan, Llandysul and Dre-fach Felindre. Dre-fach Felindre was without doubt the most important

village, with the neighbouring villages of Waungilwen, Drefelin, Cwmhiraeth and Cwm-pen-graig close behind. The villages relied entirely on the woollen industry rather than agriculture, and in common with the towns and villages of the southern Wales valleys a more urbanised outlook developed, and more urbanised pleasures sought.

It was undoubtedly the presence of water to drive the machinery and to scour and wash raw wool and fabrics that helped the area to reach prominence; in 1900 one local historian wrote of Dre-fach Felindre –

> Nearly all the power of the streams and rivers has been harnessed to drive machinery. There is hardly a spot on the banks of rivers where it would be convenient to build an additional factory or mill.

The villages were well placed both for the sheep farms and for the markets in the southern Wales valleys, and with the coming of the railway to Henllan in 1895 rapid development followed. Certain mills concentrated on particular markets, and mutual agreements with southern Wales' drapers were common,

Drefelin

Pantglas mill at Cwmhiraeth for example concentrating on Sir Fynwy (Monmouthshire) and the Rhondda valleys.

It was after 1880 that the centuries old tradition of hand weaving and knitting was transformed by mechanisation and the introduction of power looms. Labour, both locally and from afar was attracted into the area, and new mills were built. There was a distinct division of labour in the factories, with children following their parents into the mills from as early as ten. Constant work and demand for products led to an era of prosperity, with new houses replacing the old cottages, and fortunes amassed by the mill owners. However prosperity lasted for only some forty years – during the First World War wool prices reached record levels, and the Teifi provided the uniforms for front line soldiers. The end of the war in 1918 spelt disaster as prices fell, and the smaller mills closed. Building stopped, and there was an exodus to the towns. The urban structures and societies of brass bands and choirs were forced to close, as were the chapels and stores. The advocates of the new Labour party were forced to seek power in other areas. Of the fifty mills that operated in 1900 in Dre-fach Felindre twenty ceased operation. In the area as a whole, during the ten years from 1918 to 1928, of the fourteen factory mills that caught fire only two were rebuilt. The heyday was over. In 1976 the Museum of the Welsh Woollen Industry was opened at Dre-fach Felindre at the former Cambrian mill, originally built in 1912, and incorporating the working mill of Melin Teifi. It's aim is to demonstrate the history of the industry in this, it's most important region, and by it's products to demonstrate that it is still a modern and relevant industry.

2. In 1994 a project began to identify what were the buildings of the woollen industry, to clear footpaths in the area, and to set up a series of information boards and woollen trails highlighting the history of the region. The information panel at Cwm-pen-graig gives graphic representation of which properties were involved, and which aspects of the industry they specialised in.

It was at Coedmor mill in the village in the 1820's that the first water powered carding machine and spinning mules were introduced in the area. Little of the mill remains, but it's importance has given it the claim to be the origin of the modern woollen industry on the Teifi.

WALK DIRECTIONS   **[-] denotes Point of Interest**

1. Take the track parallel to the entrance to the museum **[1]**, go thorough a wooden gate, and across a bridge. After a short distance the track bears right – leave the track through a metal gate ahead, and continue on a grass track.

2. At the road turn right, passing a former mill which is now a leisure centre, on the left. At the top of the rise there is a path leading back sharply to the left. Take this and continue to reach the main road through Waungilwen.

3. Cross the road and take the track opposite. Continue to reach a stile and gate - do not cross, but bear right through Dandinas farm. Continue on the track to reach a white house, where the route continues on a footpath.

4. Shortly drop down to cross a foot-bridge, and then another – the overgrown pond to the right once acted as a header reservoir for the five mills that were powered by the stream just followed. Cross another foot-bridge and continue on the path, passing by a house – Dinas Bach.

5. At a T junction of tracks turn left – right will take you down to a ford – and continue to reach a minor road.

6. Bear right, and on meeting another minor road bear right again, and continue down to Cwmhiraeth. Just before the bridge bear left on a track signposted Troed-y-rhiw.

7. Continue to Troed-y-rhiw, and take the footpath to the left of the property, to meet a cross-roads of tracks. Continue ahead to meet a minor road.

8. Continue ahead on the minor road for a short distance, and continue, again ahead, on a track – to the right, on the skyline of Moelfre, are three wind turbines.

9. Continue downhill on the track, passing Derllys on the right, to eventually join a minor road – directly ahead is a tiled sign indicating the property of Penrhiw Fawr.

10. Turn left and continue downhill to the attractive hamlet of Cwm-pen-graig – Soar chapel, with it's imposing garden, dates from 1928 [2]. Continue uphill to join the main road into Drefach Felindre. There is an information panel next to the telephone box and bench.

11. Bear left and continue on the road, until, just after a bend in the road, and adjacent to the sign for Cwm-pen-graig on the right, there is a footpath leading right, uphill, into the trees.

12. Continue uphill through the wood – good views of the attractive houses are below to the left – to reach a stile giving access to a field. Cross the field, keeping to the right edge, to reach a minor road.

13. Bear left, and shortly leave the road through a kissing-gate on the right. Continue downhill to reach a T junction of paths – bear left to reach another kissing-gate. Cross the field to a clearly visible stone stile set in the field wall opposite, and adjacent to the road.

14. Bear right and cross the bridge leading to Drefelin. (It is worth walking on into Drefelin, before returning to the bridge. Information panel in the village). Immediately after crossing the bridge bear left onto a track, and continue alongside the river to reach a kissing-gate giving access to fields. Keeping to the right edge continue to reach a track.

15. Bear right up the track to shortly join a minor road. Bear left and continue to another road. Again bear left – there is a sign 'Welcome to Dre-fach Felindre' here. At the bottom of the road bear right to return to the starting point.

FACILITIES

Most available. Museum of the Welsh Woollen Industry.

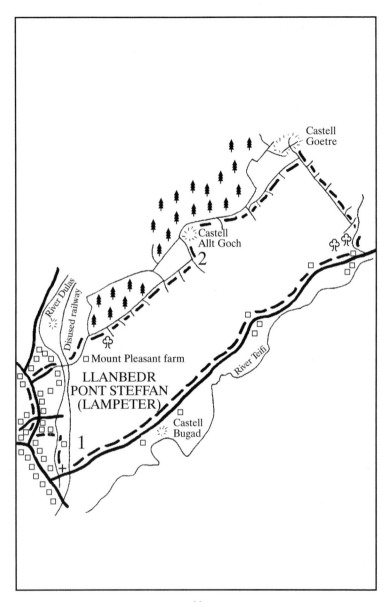

Castell Goetre

Castell Allt Goch

2

River Dulas

Disused railway

Mount Pleasant farm

LLANBEDR
PONT STEFFAN
(LAMPETER)

River Teifi

1

Castell Bugad

LAMPETER (LLANBEDR PONT STEFFAN) – CASTELL ALLT GOCH – CASTELL GOETRE – LAMPETER (LLANBEDR PONT STEFFAN)

OS Maps: 1:50 000 Lampeter and Llandovery Landranger 146; 1:25 000 Lampeter/Llanbedr Pont Steffan Explorer 199.

Start: Llanbedr Pont Steffan town centre.

Access: Llanbedr Pont Steffan, a university town, is situated on one of the main crossing points of the river Teifi, on the junctions of the A482, A475 and A485. On all major bus routes.

Parking: Any of the car parks in Llanbedr Pont Steffan.

Grade: Moderate.

POINTS OF INTEREST:

1. Llanbedr Pont Steffan's position in the landscape, and it's growth as a market town, owes much to it's strategic siting where the river Dulas flows into the river Teifi. There is no clear evidence of human settlement before the arrival of the Normans; more prominent sites were favoured by Iron Age settlers, whilst the Romans built their fort of Bremia to the north-east. However there would probably have been an early Christian site; Silian church to the north has two early inscribed Christian stones, one built into the south wall of the church, dating from the fifth or early sixth century, and gives in Latin a memorial to either Silbandus or the son of Bandus. It has been scored through by a seventh to eleventh century linear cross. The other carved stone is inside the church, dating from the ninth or tenth century. With Norman expansion into the territory came the building of motte and bailey castles as

defendable settlements. The motte (mound) in the university grounds, at the back of Dewi Sant Building, allegedly dates from the late 1080's. It was razed to the ground by the Welsh in the 1130's, and never rebuilt. To the east of the town, overlooking the river Teifi, is another motte – Castell Bugad, possibly named after Sir Hugh Buged, earl of Norfolk, active in Wales during the reign of Stephen (1135 to 1154).

Thirteenth century records note Llanbedr Pont Steffan's position as a market town for the surrounding area; by the eighteenth century Llanbedr Pont Steffan hosted eight annual fairs, as well as a weekly market – it was also an important droving centre. There was a church dedicated to St Pedr (Peter) in the town by the thirteenth century, and the old Welsh name for the town, Llanbedr Talybont Ystyfn (church of Peter near the end of Stephen's bridge) links church and bridge together, one eye on God perhaps, and the other on commerce. The bridge over the Teifi is still called Pont Steffan – perhaps linking the bridge with the reign of Stephen. The town's name in Welsh is

University and Norman motte

now Llanbedr Pont Steffan, more commonly abbreviated to Llanbed. The old medieval church was demolished in 1820 as ruinous, but it's replacement was seen as so ugly that it too was demolished, the present building not completed until 1869/1870. It's rebuilding further uphill meant that the gentry graves once snug within the church were left exposed in the new churchyard. The town council was established in 1884 when it received it's charter as a municipal borough. The town was well served by railway lines. The Manchester and Milford Railway Company was originally founded in 1846 with the idea of promoting a railway from Crewe to Aberdaugleddau (Milford Haven) via Llanbedr Pont Steffan and Llanidloes, Aberdaugleddau being promoted as an alternative port to Liverpool. Only sections of it were ever built; in 1866 the line north from Pencader to Llanbedr Pont Steffan opened, with a branch to Aberystwyth in 1867. In 1911 another line to Aberaeron on the Ceredigion coast opened – the Llanbedr Pont Steffan, Aberaeron and Newquay Light Railway. Until quite recently it was possible to walk along the track bed from Llanbedr Pont Steffan to near Betws Bledrws (to the north-east on the A485), but it has recently been fenced off.

One notable family, the Lloyds, were of considerable importance in the history of the town, holding at one time the lordship of Llanbedr Pont Steffan. They provided a Principal of Jesus College, Oxford, plus numerous local judges and MPs. Fortunes declined from the seventeenth century onwards however, when they were involved in an infamous murder when one Samuel Pritchard, a friend of the family, was discovered to have been having an affair with one of the ladies of their mansion (Maesyfelin), whether a servant or otherwise is not known. One night he was smothered with a pillow by several of the men, put in a sack, and his body thrown into the Tywi. They were betrayed to Pritchard's father, a local vicar, well known for religious poetry and his stern piety. He cursed them – in an English translation it ran:

The curse of god on Maesyfelin fall
On root of every tree, on stone of every wall
Because the flower of fair Llanymddyfri town
Was headlong cast in Tywi's flood to drown.

No trace now remains of Maesyfelin.

Llanbedr Pont Steffan has the distinction of being the smallest university in Europe, with some two thousand students, and the greater distinction of being the third oldest in England and Wales after Oxford and Cambridge. It was founded by Thomas Burgess, Bishop of Tyddewi (St David's), who from 1804 gathered funds to found a college for those Welsh students who were financially unable to attend Oxbridge colleges. He had intended the site to be at nearby Llanddewibrefi, with it's strong associations with Welsh Christianity, but he was given land in Llanbedr Pont Steffan at Castle field, and the foundation stone was laid in 1822. It opened, appropriately enough, on Dydd Gŵyl Dewi (St David's Day) 1827. The designer was Charles Cockerell, who modelled it on the Oxbridge colleges – his original building is now known as Dewi Sant's (St David's) Building, though formerly it was just the Old Building. It's cost was £16,204 6s 7d, a vast sum for the time. Originally the aim of the college was to train young men for the Church, but inevitably to survive it has had to widen it's choices over the years. In 1971 it became a full college of the federal University of Wales; in 1996 changing it's title from Dewi Sant's University College to the University of Wales, Llanbedr Pont Steffan. The Chancellor of the University of Wales is Prince Charles. Visitors are welcome to walk around the campus.

2. Of the two Iron Age forts on the walk Castell Goetre is much the larger, well over twice the size of Castell Allt Goch – the name Goetre derives from the Welsh 'coetref', meaning woodland or homestead, and Allt Goch, from 'gallt' (hill or wood) and 'coch' (red). Both date from the late first millennium BC, and would have been defendable homesteads, their banks

and ditches offering protection, and with a wooden palisade built around the earthen bank for further defence. The settlers would have made their living by cereal production and by the herding of cattle and sheep, the forts providing shelter for animals and humans. Some evidence has been found of huts and gateways, but over the centuries constant ploughing has obliterated most traces. Castell Allt Goch's single bank is still in good condition, it's oval enclosure still discernible, and covering some 1.4 hectares. The entrance was probably on the western side, and may have acted as entrance to both an earlier, smaller enclosure, and the later fort. Castell Goetre covers nearly four hectares, but it's absorption into five fields makes it appear initially much smaller. Like Allt Goch it has a single bank and ditch. There is another Iron Age fort, Castell Olwen, by the disused railway line just to the north-west of Mount Pleasant farm.

WALK DIRECTIONS   **[-] denotes Point of Interest**

1. Starting from Llanbedr Pont Steffan **[1]** town centre – that is the junction of the A475 and A482 – walk along College Road, passing the university on the right, and continue on the A482/A485 Aberaeron and Tregaron road. Passing the war memorial to the left continue to reach a rugby field on the right. Bear right on the road/bridleway adjacent, and continue on to Mount Pleasant farm. Just before the farm entrance bear left, and keeping the farm building walls to the right continue to gain a track through woodland.

2. On reaching a cross-roads of paths continue ahead over a stile – the stile left will take you into Olwen wood. Continue across fields, keeping the woodland to your immediate left. On reaching the end of the wood continue ahead through an avenue of trees to reach a gate and stile – there is an old stone gate-post here with a hole through the top of the stone.

3. Bear left. The banks of Castell Allt Goch **[2]** are clearly defined – the chimney visible in the distance is the nineteenth century,

now ruinous, folly tower on the Derry Ormond estate close by Betws Bledrws on the A485. At the bottom of the field bear right and continue ahead, again keeping the woodland to your left.

4. Continue ahead, moving away from the woodland, across V shaped and ladder stiles, to reach a stile and gate and stone gate-post. The route now bears right, but it is worth bearing left to visit Castell Goetre – the site is deceptive, the banks of the fort incorporated into five fields make it's original size difficult to determine. The modern enclosure is a small reservoir.

5. From Castell Goetre return to gate and stile and continue across fields keeping to the right edge. On entering the sixth field bear to the right and follow the edge of the wood down to gain a stile giving access to the track to Penlanmedd. There is a good view of the river Teifi ahead. Bear right and continue down to the minor road.

6. Bear right and continue on the minor road, passing the Norman motte of Castell Bugad by Castle farm, to reach the outskirts of Llanbedr Pont Steffan by Brondeifi chapel. Next to the chapel, and before the bridge, bear right on a footpath alongside the river Dulas. Continue to reach the University campus. Cross the river by a foot-bridge and continue through the campus to reach the centre of town and the starting point.

FACILITIES
All available in town.

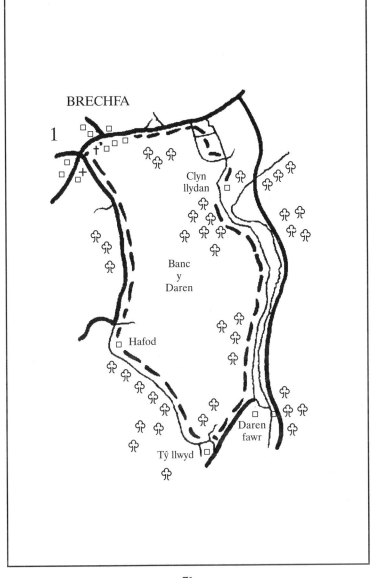

BRECHFA

1

Clyn
llydan

Banc
y
Daren

Hafod

Daren
fawr

Tŷ llwyd

BRECHFA – HAFOD – TŶ LLWYD – DAREN FAWR – CLYN LLYDAN – BRECHFA

OS Maps: 1:50 000 Lampeter and Llandovery Landranger
              146; 1:25 000 Llandeilo & Brechfa Forest/Fforest
              Brechfa Explorer 186.
Start: Brechfa.
Access: Brechfa is 6 miles north of the A40 at Nantgaredig,
              on the B4310. Bus 282 Brechfa – Caerfyrddin
              (Carmarthen) Monday to Saturday, Bus 283
              Llandeilo – Brechfa – Caerfyrddin Wednesdays
              and Saturdays only.
Parking: Car park in Brechfa – at Victoria Park close by the
              Forest Arms.
Grade: Moderate – steep initial section.

POINTS OF INTEREST:

1. The destiny of Brechfa village and forest have often been tied
together. The present Brechfa forest, a rather sprawling affair, is
Forestry Commission land, and there has been conifer planting
from the late 1920s onwards. The original forest would have
been deciduous, with some clearance during Neolithic and
Roman times. During the Norman period the Forest of
Glyncothi, as it was then known, stretched from the middle
reaches of the river Cothi to the river Teifi. It played a central
role in the defence of Welsh Deheubarth (modern day
Ceredigion, Sir Gaerfyrddin and Sir Benfro (Pembrokeshire),
together with Gŵyr (Gower)) against Norman encroachment.
The forest provided shelter, and a base for the Welsh to conduct
a guerilla war. It was not until the thirteenth century Edwardian
campaign to settle and pacify Wales that systematic clearance
took place; special woodsmen, well guarded, formed part of his

army, and they were responsible for clearing routes and providing timber. With the ascendancy of the Norman Marcher lords hunting forests were established, which included large open tracts of heath. The village became wealthy by toll collection, and by accompanying the hunting nobility, and by providing accommodation for noble and Royal hunters.

From the 15th century onwards there was increasing loss of forestry to agriculture. However enough remained over the centuries for local wood to be used in the production of naphtha for the explosives industry during the First World War. During the 1930s a camp was built by the Ministry of Labour for unemployed workers from valleys of southern Wales, providing accommodation whilst they were involved in building roads for the Forestry Commission. During the Spanish Civil War it was used to house Basque refugee children. The church was built during the late nineteenth/early twentieth century fashion for the (much needed) restoration of churches, and incorporated

River Cothi

parts of the older dilapidated building. The triple bellcote was filled after 1918, incorporating the bell from the old church, a new bell from a chemical works, and another purpose made. The site dates back to the sixth century, and the original church established by St Teilo. There have been several colourful characters associated with Brechfa church and village over the years – one Thomas Glyn Cothi, a noted Unitarian minister born in the village in 1764, gained himself a prison term for his outspoken support for the radicalism of the French Revolution, and the abolition of slavery. Brechfa can be translated as 'mottled place', a place showing irregular blotches of various colours, and suggestive of the autumnal colours of a deciduous forest. However eleventh and twelfth century documents in the Llyfr Llandaf (Book of Llandaf) note the parish name as Bracma.

WALK DIRECTIONS   **[-] denotes Point of Interest**
1. Starting from the car park in Brechfa [1] turn right to shortly turn left on to the road opposite the Forest Arms hotel. If the ford is too high to cross retrace your steps to the main road, turn left and cross the bridge, and then turn left, passing in front of the chapel, to gain the other side of the river.
2. Continue uphill on the minor road, ignoring the footpath left opposite Llwyn Griffith. Eventually the road levels out, and where the road bends sharp right leave through a farm gate to enter a field.
3. Follow a well defined track, initially running by the right-hand side of the hedge, and where it bends left, passing in front of the ruins of Hafod, continue downhill to reach the farm of Tŷ Llwyd.
4. Go through the farmyard and turn left on the minor road leading to Daren Fawr. Just before Daren Fawr turn left to gain the path leading alongside the river Cothi. From July to October the river bank is full of the purple-pinks of Himalayan balsam, edging the path and river.
5. Follow the path to reach the ruins of Clyn Llydan. Follow the

distinct path which passes around the back of the ruins and continue ahead on the track as it passes between fields.

6. Follow this as it bends left downhill to reach a ford. Cross by the gated footbridge to the right. Rejoin the track and turn sharply to the left to reach a stile giving access to a field.

7. Enter the field and initially bear diagonally right through the scrub to reach more open wet grassland. Aim for a post, with a County Walks disc sign on it, in the centre of the field to the left. Once reached turn sharp right, and keeping an electricity pole directly ahead, aim for a gap in the top of the field.

8. Go through the gap and aim for the top left of the field. Once at a stile cross, turn left, and follow the road back to Brechfa and the starting point.

FACILITIES

Toilets at car park. Tŷ Mawr hotel (a sixteenth century former mansion house), Forest Arms hotel, *Glasfryn* guest house, Post Office and shop. Mountain bikes can be hired from *Glasfryn* – there are waymarked cycling routes in Brechfa forest. The forest is currently also used as a stage in the (car) Rally of Great Britain, part of the FIA World Rally Championship.

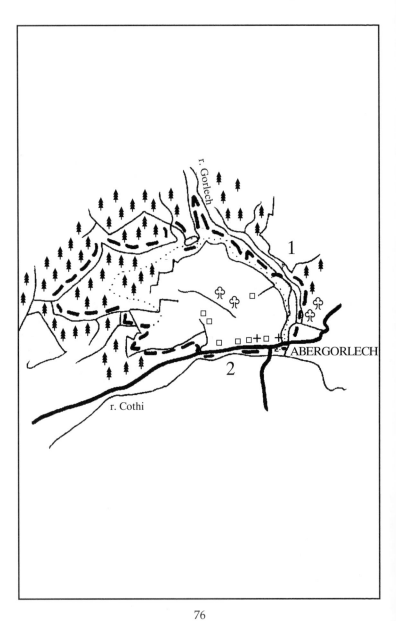

r. Gorlech

1

2

ABERGORLECH

r. Cothi

ABERGORLECH CIRCULAR

OS Maps: 1:50 000 Lampeter and Llandovery Landranger
             146; 1:25 000 Llandeilo & Brechfa Forest/Fforest
             Brechfa Explorer 186.
Start: Forestry Commission car park in Abergorlech.
Access: Abergorlech is on the B4310 between Brechfa and
             Llansawel. Bus 283 Llandeilo – Abergorlech –
             Caerfyrddin (Carmarthen) Wednesdays and
             Saturdays only.
Parking: Forestry Commission car park.
Grade: Easy – on Forestry permitted paths and tracks.

POINTS OF INTEREST:

1. Like near neighbour Brechfa, Abergorlech once formed part
of the medieval Forest of Glyncothi. Originally home to those
defending Welsh independence from Norman encroachment
the forest became, following the Edwardian victory in the late
thirteenth century, a Royal forest. A source of timber, it was also
used as a hunting reserve and as a source of hawks for falconry.
Well protected by forest law, transgressions against venison and
vert were severely punished. Venison included not only deer,
whether red, roe or fallow, but all forest animals, including
foxes, wild boars and wolves. Vert covered the trees, coppices,
the underwood and the feeding areas of all forest game. With
the Act of Union of Wales with England in 1536 it became the
Royal manor of Glyncothi, it's lands normally leased out to the
local gentry. Forest law was finally abolished in 1640. By the end
of the seventeenth century most of the old oak-wood had been
cleared.

The Forestry Commission was founded in 1919 to re-
establish depleted forests like Glyncothi. A wide range of

species were planted here from the late 1920s onwards. Of interest was the forest garden planted in the Gorlech Valley – a trial area to see which species flourished best. Like Brechfa there was a camp, nearby at Treglog, which housed unemployed workers from the southern Wales valleys who helped build the forestry roads and plant trees. Much of the success of a species depends on the altitude at which it is planted. In upland areas larch, lodgepole pine and Sitka spruce were favoured; in lowland areas Douglas fir, Western hemlock and Lawson cypress. A broad-leaved element was retained. Larch finds use in fencing and gates, Douglas fir for uses in the construction industry and, like Western hemlock, for use as pulp for paper. Western red cedar will make you strong and durable rugby posts. Broad-leaved ash has long been favoured for tool handles, and like oak and beech, finds use in furniture making. Nowadays as much emphasis is placed on recreation and conservation as on timber, if not more so. There are cycle and walk routes set out in the forests, and Brechfa forest is currently

Abergorlech

one stage in the world car rally championship.

2. In the sixteenth century Abergorlech consisted of only one dwelling house, and it was home to the local gentry, the Prices. It was the Price family who built the bridge over the Cothi, probably in the sixteenth century, to encourage those who lived south of the river to use the estate's flour mill, the ruins of which still stand close by. A carved stone in the bridge notes it's repair by a John Jones in 1794. *The Black Lion Inn* was a coaching inn in the sixteenth century, the main road and drove route at that time being the present byway running along the north bank of the Cothi, and linking Abergorlech with Rhydodyn (Edwinsford), the former gentry home of the Williams of Talyllychau (Talley). One local curiosity are the Gorlech stones, glimpsed in the front gardens of the village cottages, and having been found in the local river. Originally nodules of iron-rich mudstones they have dried out and cracked, the resultant cracks filled at a later date with calcite. The softer mudstone has partly eroded giving the stones their curious shapes and appeal – they were once thought to be fossil animals. Like the river Tywi into which it flows, the Cothi is world famous for it's salmon and sea trout.

WALK DIRECTIONS   **[-] denotes Point of Interest**

1. Starting from the car park go passed the gate giving entrance to the forest [1]. Follow, initially, the blue ringed posts, and descend left down steps and continue on the path alongside the Gorlech river. After a short distance the path turns right up the steps to rejoin the main forest track.

2. Continue along the track, to shortly take a path which drops down to the left. Cross the foot-bridge and continue on the path as it bears left and up to reach two posts and signs indicating 'Short Walk' and 'Long Walk'. Turn sharply to the right onto the 'Long Walk'. After a short distance a path joins from the left – continue ahead.

3. Where the path joins a track, turn sharp left and walk uphill.

Waymarks and blue ring post here.

4. Continue to reach a cross-roads of paths. Left will take you down to Abergorlech – go ahead, and follow the track uphill as it bears right and left to reach a cross-roads of forest-tracks. Turn left, and continue on this track – great views on the left over the Cothi Valley.

5. After approximately a mile/1.5 kilometres bear left on a distinct track. After a short distance a track leaves to the right – continue ahead and down. There are good views to the left of the route walked so far. Again, after a short distance a track bears right. Take this path – ahead would lead you to a field and a path leading downhill to the left of the field.

6. Where another track appears ahead stay left and continue down to enter a field. Bear right on the distinct track and continue on this track as it bears left and left again to lead you out on to the main B4310.

7. Turn left and continue through Abergorlech [2] to regain the starting point.

FACILITIES

Public toilets opposite the pub in the village. Picnic site at the forest car park.

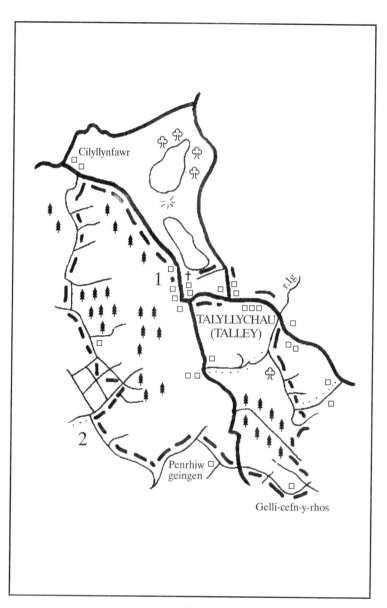

Cilyllynfawr

1

✝

r.lg

TALYLLYCHAU
(TALLEY)

2

Penrhiw
geingen

Gelli-cefn-y-rhos

TALYLLYCHAU (TALLEY) – CILYLLYNFAWR – MYNYDD CYNROS – PENRHIW GEINGEN – GELLI-CEFN-Y-RHOS – TALYLLYCHAU (TALLEY)

OS Maps: 1:50 000 Lampeter and Llandovery Landranger 146; 1:25 000 Llandeilo & Brechfa Forest / Fforest Brechfa Explorer 186.

Start: Talyllychau Abbey.

Access: Talyllychau is on the B4302 between Llandeilo and Llansawel. Buses 283 Llandeilo – Llansawel – Caerfyrddin (Carmarthen) Wednesday and Saturday, 284 Llanbedr Pont Steffan (Lampeter) – Llansawel – Llandeilo Tuesday and Friday.

Parking: By Talyllychau Abbey.

Grade: Moderate – steep section at beginning of walk.

POINTS OF INTEREST:

1. Talley is a lazy corruption of the Welsh Talyllychau which means, 'head of the lakes'. The two lakes in question were formed at the end of the Ice Age, formed by debris from the retreating ice-sheets. This peaceful and remote area proved ideal for the Premonstratensian order who established the abbey here in the late 1180s. The order was founded in 1120 by St Norbert of Xanten, who established, with thirteen companions, the first monastery at Prémontré in France. Like the Cistercians they adopted the white habit; however whilst they based their constitution on the Cistercian and their life of rural simplicity and labour, they added the Augustinian belief in service to the community. Their motto was devotion, scholarship and service, and in addition to the abbot and monks there were ordained canons who went out to administer the sacrament in local churches.

The abbey itself was founded by the Lord Rhys, Rhys ap Gruffudd, who endowed it with lands both close by, and further afield in Gwent, Gŵyr (*Gower*) and Ceredigion. At Talyllychau upland granges were given over to cattle, and in particular sheep, with lowland granges to cereals, accompanied by clearance of the native woodland. Whilst there were several Premonstratensian abbeys in Scotland and England, Talyllychau was the order's only abbey in Wales. It seems to have had a fairly impoverished history, partly caused by it's remoteness, and either war, or neglect by it's abbots, and it was taken under Royal control on a number of occasions. In 1284 the abbey was under investigation for loose-living, the canons threatened by Edward I with expulsion and replacement by those 'of the English tongue who are able and willing to observe the religious life'. Again in 1433 it was noted that it's possessions had been 'wasted by misrule'. Canons from English houses had to be transferred to Talyllychau to remedy affairs.

With dissolution in 1536 a new church was created by

Talyllychau Abbey

walling off the transepts, aisles and western half of the nave of the abbey church. However by 1722 it had become unsafe and a new one was built close by in the following year, using abbey stone. The abbey buildings were left to decay and became a useful quarry for the village. The ruined tower, however, still dominates the area. The church, dedicated to St Mary, still contains the original box pews, numbered and graded for the local gentry family, the Williams of Rhydodyn (Edwinsford), their tenants and retainers. Whilst the church is normally locked they are easily glimpsed through the windows. There is no access to the lakes; the lower, furthest from the church, is a nature reserve under the management of the Wildlife Trust of South and West Wales – they give occasional guided walks. The mound between the two lakes is the remains of a possibly Welsh motte and bailey castle.

Talyllychau vies with the ruined abbey of Ystrad-fflur (Strata Florida) in Ceredigion as the last resting place of one of Wales' finest national poets, Dafydd ap Gwilym. Both sites have their advocates, though Dafydd is known to have spent his last years here in Talyllychau. Through his poetry he presented a self portrait of himself, and of Welsh and English society of mid fourteenth century Wales, whether his themes were of landscape and the natural world, of everyday life and religion, or of the misadventures that befell him. In 'Trafferth mewn Tafarn' (Trouble at a Tavern) he paints an ironic portrait of himself as he fails to keep an assignation with a girl – in the process of trying to reach her room he wakes and annoys everyone, and frightens three Englishmen who fear they will be robbed:

> When at last, wretched journey!
> All did sleep, save her and me,
> I to reach the lady's bed
> Most skilfully attempted.
> But I fell …

On a table-top my forehead,
Where, all the time a pitcher
And a loud brass cauldron were.
Collapse of that stout table –
Two trestles downed – stools as well!
Cry that the cauldron uttered
Behind me, for miles was heard …

2. Rich as were the views of mid Wales on the ascent to Mynydd Cynros, now ahead are stretched out the tight lines of the Bannau Brycheiniog (Brecon Beacons) and Sir Gaerfyrddin (Carmarthenshire) Fan. The green lane ahead (and also part of the route just walked) was one of the many drover's roads in the area; cattle, sheep and pigs were taken from local farms to local markets, some destined for England's towns. This lane will take you to Abergorlech. Mynydd Cynros, until enclosure within straight well defined boundaries in 1817, was Talyllychau Common, providing common pasture for local freeholders.

WALK DIRECTIONS   **[-] denotes Point of Interest**
1. Starting from the car park by the abbey **[1]** walk up the road, ignoring the first signposted path leading uphill left through trees, to pass Talyllychau's lakes on your right. Just before Cilyllynfawr, turn left through a gate to enter a field. There is a walking man footpath sign here.
2. Keeping the stream and hedge to your immediate right continue uphill across fields and stiles, and through bracken, to finally reach an even level. There are plenty of opportunities to pause and admire the views on the ascent!
3. Once on the level continue across this field, to the forest boundary edge ahead to meet a gate and stile. Continue ahead, crossing a foot-bridge and stile, and keeping the forest on your immediate left.
4. Where the forest swings left and downhill keep to the line of

the hedge as it bears right to pass the ruins of Blaen Cwm Yr Efail. This once prosperous farm was home to Sir William Davies, a former editor of the *Western Mail*, Wales' English language daily newspaper. Continue to reach a stile in the corner of the field.

5. Cross the stile and continue diagonally right across the field to a stile in the hedge opposite. Cross and turn diagonally left to reach another stile in the bottom right of the field, just to the left of a boggy section.

6. Cross, and turn right to pass a waymarked post. Take the stile on the bottom right (left will take you back to Talyllychau), and continue on an overgrown green lane. This lane shortly enters a open field. Keep to the right edge to meet a gate giving access to a green lane [2].

7. Do not enter the lane but bear left, and with the hedge on your right continue downhill, crossing a stile *en route* until, where the hedge bends to the right by a gate at the bottom of a field, bear left. There is a waymarked post here. Continue, keeping the hedge to your right, and crossing a stile on the way, reach a gate, a stile and another waymarked post.

8. Turn right and follow the track as it passes the farm of Penrhiw Geingen on the right. There are good views of the lakes below left before the farm is reached. Continue passed the farm, and where another track leads off to the right keep left, and continue to reach a minor road. Left will take you back downhill to Talyllychau.

9. Cross the road and go through the gate into the field opposite. Keep the hedge to your left to cross by a stile and gate at the bottom of the field into another field ahead and slightly right. Waymark sign here. Continue downhill, again keeping the hedge to your left, to reach a track.

10. Turn left and follow the track through the farmyard of Gelli-Cefn-y-Rhos, an outstanding example of a late medieval farmhouse of formerly thatched long farmhouse and joined former byre, to join a green lane. Continue to reach a corrugated

iron shed, bearing left and continuing on a narrow track. Good views right over the farm below and the lands towards Talyllychau and beyond.

11. Continue to reach a well defined forestry track. Cross the track and directly ahead continue on a path going downhill through scrub. After a short distance reach a gate and stile. Cross by stile and after a short distance, before reaching the trees ahead, meet a waymarked post directing you right and downhill. Go steeply downhill to reach a stile. Bear right on a track to reach a foot-bridge over the river Ig.

12. Cross and bear left, keeping the river to your left, to reach a gate and stile giving access to a track which passes the treatment works on the left. Continue to a T junction. Bear left, and just before reaching a bridge over the river Ig, bear right by a stile.

13. Continue ahead, until after crossing a foot-bridge and stile bear diagonally right to shortly top a rise by a clump of trees. Keeping the undergrowth and river on the left go ahead, looping around fence posts by the river's edge, to reach a foot-bridge across the river.

14. Do not cross the foot-bridge but bear right, keeping the field hedge to your left, to reach a gate giving access to a track. Turn right and continue to reach the main road. Bear left and continue to either bear left at the first left turn to reach the starting point, or continue on the main road and take the path leading off left alongside the lake to the churchyard and start.

FACILITIES

Post office and pub/restaurant in village. Public toilets just passed the abbey. The abbey is open all year, no charge. Good pub in Cwm-du village due south of Talyllychau, but only open Wednesdays and Saturdays 19.00 to 23.00 hours! Dolau cothi Roman Gold Mines to the north-east at Pumpsaint, are also well worth a visit – there is a pub in Pumpsaint and a visitor centre with information on the red kite.

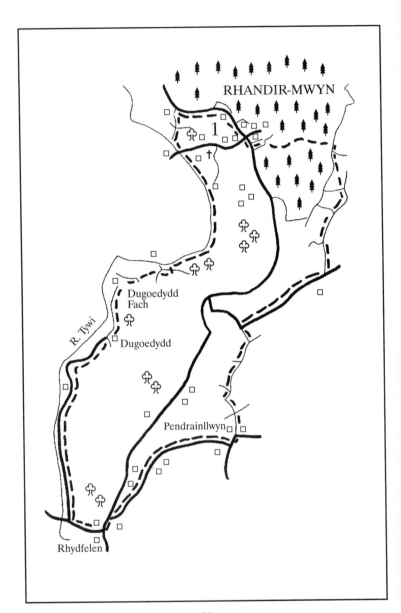

RHANDIR-MWYN

1

Dugoedydd
Fach

R. Tywi

Dugoedydd

Pendrainllwyn

Rhydfelen

RHANDIR-MWYN – PENDRAINLLWYN – RHYDFELEN – DUGOEDYDD – DUGOEDYDD FACH - RHANDIR-MWYN

OS Maps: 1:50 000 Lampeter and Llandovery Landranger
146, Brecon Beacons Landranger 160, Elan Valley
and Builth Wells Landranger 147; 1:25 000
Llandovery/Llanymddyfri Explorer 187.

Start: *Royal Oak Inn* at Rhandir-mwyn.

Access: Rhandir-mwyn is 7 miles from Llanymddyfri
(Llandovery) on the minor road north to Llyn
Brianne. There is a Postbus service 287 which
operates from Llanymddyfri to Rhandir-mwyn on
selected days during the week, but it is a slow
service.

Parking: Limited parking on the road by the *Royal Oak Inn.*

Grade: Strenuous.

POINTS OF INTEREST:

1. Situated in the upper Tywi Valley amongst the foothills of the
Cambrian Mountains, Rhandir-mwyn is one of the most
captivating areas of Wales. The river Tywi, which flows fast and
cold through the valley has divided more than land in it's
history; to the east lay the medieval lordship of Cantref Bychan,
and to the west, between the rivers Tywi and Teifi, the lordship
of Cantref Mawr. Circa 1200 the northern section of Cantref
Bychan was granted as a grange to the Cistercian monks of
Ystrad-fflur (Strata Florida), the area becoming known in later
years as Rhandir Abbot, 'rhandir' meaning a share of land. In
time the name Rhandir overlapped with the locality of Nant-y-
mwyn to the south to become by the early nineteenth century
Rhandir-mwyn.

Nant-y-mwyn (the mineral stream) was also the name given to the old mansion built by the ancestors of the Earl of Cawdor, and it was the Cawdors who, by the end of the eighteenth century, had become the principal landowners in the area. Lead mining had probably been begun by the Romans, and later the Cistercians, and the Cawdors followed, opening up the area to provide ore for the lead works they had established in Caerfyrddin (Carmarthen) circa 1760. Between 1775 and 1797 nearly 30,000 tons of lead were extracted, with the help of some four hundred employees, a considerable enterprise for the formerly isolated area, and the most productive in the mine's history. A considerable number of miners immigrated from Cornwall, causing some friction in the search for jobs in the leaner years of the nineteenth century. Indeed by 1836 a Cornish company had taken over control of the mine. The mine may have closed for a while during the 1880s, only to re-open and continue in production under different companies until final closure in 1931-2. Much of the mine workings in the area are now hidden by late twentieth century forestry, but the industrial workings and spoil dumps are still there to be found, as are the worker's cottages and chapels, set in amongst the irregular field patterns and scattered farms.

TWM SIÔN CATI

Twm Siôn Cati, sixteenth century outlaw and hero to countless generations of Welsh children and adults, was born in Tregaron circa 1530, the illegitimate son of a local landowner. His mother, Catherine Jones, christened him Thomas Jones, but his lack of a legitimate father gained him the name Twm Sion Cati (Tom Jones, son of Cathy). To save his mother from poverty he turned outlaw at eighteen, redistributing goods to others he deemed worthy of help. Disguise and style were part of his way of life, and he would disguise both himself and the animals he stole. He would dye a stolen bull a different colour, add a false tail, and sell it back to the original owner. One tale tells of when a tricked farmer called at his mother's cottage,

Twm, who had been warned of his coming, dressed down in rags and sat outside the cottage door. The gullible farmer, not recognising him, tossed him his silver whip, asking him to look after his horse. Twm dutifully rode the horse home to the farmer's wife, showed her the whip as token, and explained to the wife her husband had need of £50. After it was handed over Twm rode off to London to enjoy the proceeds.

When chased he and his companions would seek refuge in a cave above the river Tywi – the cave is still there, above the gorge of what is now the Royal Society for the Protection of Birds' (RSPB) nature reserve at Dinas. Though the roof has fallen in, making it more a shelter than a refuge, it can still be visited. Old age brought respectability to Twm. In 1559 he bought himself a pardon, and turned to music, poetry (often his exploits in verse), and genealogical history. He became a well respected citizen, a Justice of the Peace, and mayor of nearby Aberhonddu (Brecon) town. In 1607, age 77, he married Joan, widow of Thomas Williams of Ystradffin (close by his cave where he had kept watch over the years), daughter of the local sheriff – she was 65. Twm died some two years later, his wife Joan going on to marry the uncle of the Earl of Essex, Elizabeth I's ill fated lover. Twm's will of 17 May, 1609 is still extant; he left nine head of cattle (presumably his) to an illegitimate son, and everything else to his wife.

Anyone wishing to trace Twm's cave can find the path to it leading off the main path around the RSPB reserve. It is close by several steep steps leading down (or up), and behind a waymarked post with a white arrow, skirting a flat slab of rock. Keep going more or less straight up – there is plenty of graffiti in the cave to let you know when found, some dating back to the 1830's. Grid reference 786 466.

No visit to the area would be complete without a trip to the RSPB reserve at Dinas, 3.5 miles/5.5 kilometres north of Rhandir-mwyn. A 2 mile/3.25 kilometre trail runs around the reserve, alongside the Tywi for part of it's length, and through alder, oak, birch and rowan wood. It is at the junction of the rivers Doethïe and Tywi, and is famous as having been the last stronghold of the red kite before it's successful re-introduction into Britain. A graceful hunter, with slim long wings, a long forked tail, and plumage a mixture of chestnut and red, they are common sitings. The Kite Country Project was established in 1994 to provide public information, and to encourage visitors, with a number of feeding stations set up where it is possible to see the bird in close proximity – indeed mid Wales has now become known as Kite Country. Just north of Dinas is Llyn Brianne dam and storage reservoir. Built in 1971-2 an industrial hydropower station has been added, opening in January 1997. It provides drinking water to southern Wales, from Cydweli on the Sir Gaerfyrddin coast to the outskirts of Cardiff. As part of it's construction the mountain road on to Tregaron was upgraded, opening the country up to walkers and visitors.

Rhandir-mwyn

WALK DIRECTIONS

1. Starting from the *Royal Oak Inn* in Rhandir-mwyn, **[1]** walk passed the Post Office and shop on the left until shortly, just passed Gorof Melyn cottage, turn left through a metal gate, go ahead, and cross a stile. Continue ahead to the forest.

2. At the forest boundary cross a stile to the right, and continue on the path uphill, crossing a stile *en route*, and keeping an earthen bank to your right, reach a fire-break by a small bank of stones.

3. Bear left uphill along the fire-break. There are good views left of the valley below. Keep an eye out for the path which is to the right and just below the ridge of the fire-break, leading off through ferns. If you continue to reach the end of the fire-break you have gone too far.

4. Continue uphill on the forest path to reach a stream by a fallen tree – there is a waymark here, indicating right turn. Cross the stream as indicated, go ahead for a short distance, and then pick up the path on the left going uphill to reach another fire-break. Bear left to reach a forest track.

5. Ahead is a gate giving access to the now closed youth hostel. Bear right to reach a gate. Go through onto open country, and keeping the forestry fence to your right, continue to the corner of the fence. Follow the track and marker posts across to reach a gate.

6. Go through the gate, and keeping the fence to your left, continue on a green track as it descends, bearing to the right *en route*, to reach sheep pens. Enter the field ahead, and keeping to the right edge, descend to reach a gate giving access to a minor road. There is a good walking man sign here.

7. Bear right, and continue until where the road bears sharp right leave left through a gate, and continue ahead on a bridleway. Just before the track enters a field bear right onto a green lane. Continue ahead as it enters a field, and keeping to the left edge go ahead until it again becomes a green lane, until it reaches a corner of a field by a broken walking man sign.

8. Bear left, and keeping to the right edge continue to reach a gate and a green lane. Continue on the green lane to reach the attractive property of Pendrainllwyn. Bear right onto a minor road, and again right at the junction shortly ahead. Continue on the minor road for a mile/1.5 kilometres or so until the road to Rhandir-mwyn is reached.

9. Bear left, and then shortly right, and continue on a minor road signposted Cil-y-cwm, passing Rhydfelen *en route*, to reach the 'No Through' road to Dugoedydd just before the bridge across the river Tywi. Bear right onto the 'No Through' road and continue for over a mile/1.5 kilometres to reach Dugoedydd.

10. Turn left onto a track in front of the farm and follow it to Dugoedydd Fach. Cross a stile adjacent to the property on the right, and keeping to the left edge, continue to reach the back of the house. Ignore the small gate into the field; continue ahead across a grassy field, keeping to the left edge, to reach a stile in the corner of the field.

11. Enter the new field, and cross it diagonally right to reach a stile in the right hedge giving access to woodland. Cross and bear diagonally left uphill through the wood to reach a stile – if you stay on the lower path to the left to reach a fence you will have a short steep climb up to meet the stile.

12. Cross the stile and gain a grassy track. After a short distance cross a stile on the left and descend the steps to reach a track. Bear right, and after a short distance descend the steps on the left to reach a stile giving access to a field – the steps may be partially obscured by ferns.

13. Bear right, and keeping to the river's edge, follow paths and stiles as the path sometimes edges the river, and sometimes bears along the left edge of fields. Continue for over a mile/1.5 kilometres, to reach the camp-site and the minor road bearing right uphill to Rhandir-mwyn.

14. Cross the road by two stiles close to the bridge, and continue into the field opposite. (Across the bridge, further along the road on the left, is an old hollow oak tree – it reputedly dates

from the twelfth century, which makes it Sir Gaerfyrddin's oldest tree). Keeping to the left edge continue to the first fence. Bear right by a walking man sign, and staying in the field and keeping the fence on the left, continue to reach a stile.

15. Cross and take the path up and slightly left. Continue across a track to gain a stile adjacent to a garden on the left. Cross to the gate and bear right uphill on a track leading up to the main road back into Rhandir-mwyn – there is a property sign here reading 'Salem'. Bear right and continue along the road back to Rhandir-mwyn and the *Royal Oak Inn*.

FACILITIES

Inn and Post Office/shop in village, camp-site by river.

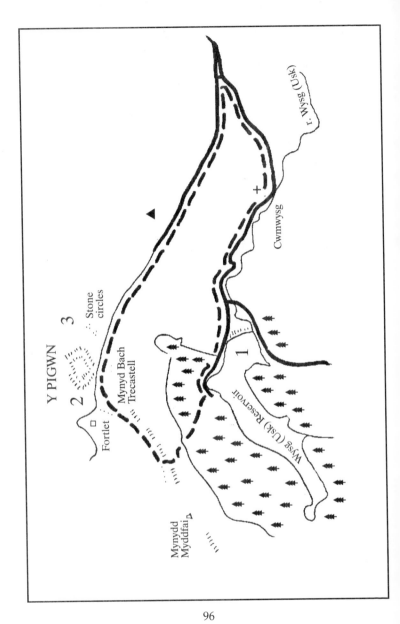

Y PIGWN

2

3

Stone circles

Fortlet

Mynyd Bach Trecastell

Mynydd Myddfai

1

Wysg (Usk) Reservoir

Cwmwysg

r. Wysg (Usk)

WYSG *(USK)* RESERVOIR – GLASFYNYDD FOREST – MYNYDD BACH TRECASTELL – Y PIGWN – CERRIG Y PIGWN – CWMWYSG – WYSG RESERVOIR

OS Maps: 1:50 000 Brecon Beacons Landranger 160; 1:25 000 Brecon Beacons Western Area Outdoor Leisure 12.

Start: Wysg Reservoir. The walk is best enjoyed in clear weather, owing to the superb views on offer.

Access: The reservoir is to the west of Trecastell on the A40 Aberhonddu (Brecon) to Llanymddyfri (Llandovery) main road.

Parking: At the reservoir.

Grade: Moderate.

POINTS OF INTEREST:

1. The Wysg reservoir is an attractive stretch of water, backed by forestry and high moorland. Opened in 1955 after five years work it takes it's name from the infant river Wysg, which rises to the south, below Fan Foel on the Caerfyrddin (Carmarthen) Mynydd Du (Black Mountain), and defines in it's passage to the reservoir the boundary between Sir Gaerfyrddin and Powys. The English name Usk derives from the Welsh 'wysg', meaning water, the same source as the Irish uisge or whiskey; this malt however supplies Swansea with drinking water. The river gathers force to eventually enter the Môr Hafren (Bristol Channel) by Casnewydd (Newport). Much emphasis these days is placed on the recreational facilities afforded by reservoirs – the Wysg is no exception. It is one of the best trout fisheries in Wales, it's natural supply of brown trout supplemented by re-stocking of both brown and rainbow trout. Fly fishing by boat, and canoeing are welcomed, but bookings must be in advance.

The fishing season runs from March to October, with day tickets available on site. There are both walking and cycle trails around the reservoir, with access into Glasfynydd forest.

2. Situated at the highest point of the old Roman road that crosses Mynydd Bach Trecastell, Y Pigwn (the peaks) is the site of two Roman marching camps. These were typically set up during military campaigns, and were built by the soldiers themselves for short stays or overnight defence. Using iron entrenching tools as a spade an encampment ditch was dug, the earth forming a defensive bank which was then topped with palisade spikes they carried with them. Their entrances were protected by curving banks. Accommodation would have been within leather tents. At Y Pigwn there are two camps, both characteristically in a playing card shape, a smaller later camp being superimposed on top of the larger. The ramparts of both camps survive, now seen as grassy banks, and are best glimpsed on the approach to the camps from the Mynydd Myddfai direction. The camps and Roman road probably date from the military campaigns to subdue the Silures during the governorship of Julius Frontinus from AD 74-8. It is Frontinus

Wysg reservoir

who is credited with planning the roads of Wales, which along with forts and marching camps formed part of his strategy of subjugation. The earlier camp here, at some fifteen hectares, is contemporary with another eighteen hectares camp at Arosfa, by the side of the minor road from Trecastell to Cross Inn, to the south of the reservoir. Arosfa would have been capable of housing almost a full legion. The Roman road would have connected the permanent fort at Llanymddyfri with that of Y Gaer near Aberhonddu (built circa AD 75). It would no doubt also have seen shipments of gold from the gold mines of Dolau cothi, protected by another fort at Pumpsaint to the north of Llanymddyfri. In the nineteenth century this road was used by the stagecoaches, oxen pulling the coaches up the incline on the Llanymddyfri side. There was an inn sited on the road, the Black Cock, which served travellers, but all traces of it have vanished – early maps show it close to Hafod Fawr, after the descent to Llanymddyfri. Early winter would have seen processions of brightly painted red Cardi (Cardigan) carts, carrying produce from Sir Benfro (Pembrokeshire), Sir Gaerfyrddin and Ceredigion to the industrial towns of southern Wales, in particular to Merthyr Tydfil. Hams, eggs, bacon, vegetables and slaughtered pigs found their way across the moorland. Farmers were wise to travel in groups of twelve or more; one solitary Ceredigion farmer was murdered for his money. Strings of mules laden with full panniers also made the trip, the panniers filled with coal for the return journey. The road too was an important drove route, as was the track across Mynydd Myddfai from the south-west. Llanymddyfri in the eighteenth and nineteenth centuries became the centre for cattle drovers, who would meet in the local inns before heading off. One can see why the site was chosen by the Romans, it commands superb views of the Caerfyrddin Fans, Fforest Fawr and the Bannau Brycheiniog (Brecon Beacons), with, to the north, Mynydd Epynt and the Cambrian Mountains. Close to where the road zigzags downhill there is another Roman fortlet, perhaps acting as a signal station.

3. A short distance from the camps are two stone circles, dating from the late Neolithic/early Bronze Age. Known as Cerrig Y Pigwn (the Peak Stones) the smaller of the two is some 24 feet/7.5 metres in diameter, with some five stones remaining, the larger at 76 feet/23 metres diameter has some twenty stones with two outliers – the central mound is probably natural. Originally the stones would have been higher and more numerous, though they are still clearly visible, set close to the fence boundary. Stone circles acted as ceremonial structures, answering the need of the then new religion's concern with the rising and setting of the sun, and the need to align their structures to it – to the south-east of the main circle is a recumbent stone aligned to the midwinter sunrise. The area is dotted with Bronze Age burial cairns, sited on the high ground; Tomen Y Rhos on Mynydd Myddfai, and marked on the OS map, is one such.

WALK DIRECTIONS   [-] denotes Point of Interest

1. Starting from the reservoir [1] continue on the tarmac road to almost reach a small parking bay at the end of the road. At the last corner before this car park take a forestry path on the right. It is set in the gap between two posts, both of which have fence wire wrapped around them. If you are at a clearly defined forestry track with a barrier, opposite the car park, then you have gone just too far.

2. Continue uphill on the path, keeping ahead, to reach a green metal gate. The old stile to the left has now collapsed, but go ahead through the gate to gain open moorland. Continue ahead on a track to cross a ford. Just passed here the path crosses an intermittent embankment which runs for some 3 miles/4.75 kilometres at the foot of the hill. The bank and ditch on the left are particularly impressive here. The earthwork is probably the remains of an eighteenth/nineteenth century stone tile quarry –

the tiles used for roofing farm buildings and houses.

3. Just passed the embankment the path divides – bear right and continue for a mile/1.5 kilometres or so along the side of the hill, keeping the embankment below right, to reach the old Roman road by a Bannau Brycheiniog National Park post. Above are the Roman marching camps of Y Pigwn [2]. Bear right and continue, passing the Neolithic/early Bronze Age stone circles of Cerrig Y Pigwn [3] to reach a gate and stile.

4. Cross the stile and continue on the road, with superb views ahead of the Bannau Brycheiniog, for a mile/1.5 kilometres, to bear right, and then right again onto the minor road leading to the reservoir. Continue on this road, passing through Cwmwysg, to regain the starting point.

FACILITIES
Nearest at Trecastell.

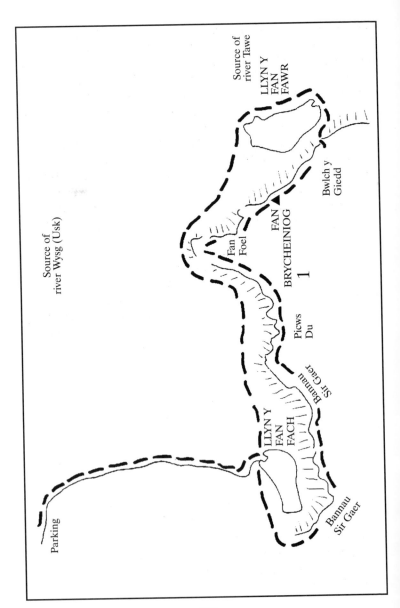

Source of river Tawe

LLYN Y FAN FAWR

Bwlch y Giedd

Source of river Wysg (Usk)

Fan Foel

FAN BRYCHEINIOG

1

Picws Du

Bannau Sir Gaer

LLYN Y FAN FACH

Parking

Bannau Sir Gaer

102

LLYN Y FAN FACH – BANNAU SIR GAER (PICWS DU) – FAN FOEL – FAN BRYCHEINIOG – BWLCH Y GIEDD – LLYN Y FAN FAWR – LLYN Y FAN FACH

OS Maps: 1:50 000 Brecon Beacons Landranger 160; 1:25 000 Brecon Beacons Western Area Outdoor Leisure 12.

Start: The parking area at the end of the road from Llanddeusant. The walk can also be joined from the minor road between Trecastell and the A4067 at Tafarn-y-Garreg.

Access: Follow the minor road from Llanddeusant, continuing ahead on an unmetalled track where the tarmac section bends right to a farm.

Parking: Rough parking passed the mountain rescue post marked on the Outdoor Leisure map, and just before the bridge carrying the path leading up to the lake.

Grade: Strenuous.

POINTS OF INTEREST:

1. The Black Mountain, often called by it's Welsh name of Mynydd Du, is that section of the Bannau Brycheiniog (Brecon Beacons) National Park which stretches from the minor top of Tair Cairn Uchaf in the west to it's Sir Gaerfyrddin (Carmarthenshire) culmination in Bannau Sir Gaer, and at Picws Du (Black Peak), the summit above Llyn y Fan Fach. It forms part of the escarpment running from Tafarn-y-Garreg on the A4067 west to Llanddeusant. Half in Sir Gaerfyrddin, half in Powys, the escarpment, known as the Carmarthen Fan or Fan Caerfyrddin (fan or ban meaning peak or beacon), is one of the finest ridge walks in Wales. Fan Foel marks the boundary point. At 2632

feet/802 metres Fan Brycheiniog in Powys is it's highest point.

The Fan Caerfyrddin itself forms part of the great Old Red Sandstone belt which runs on to the Bannau Brycheiniog and Mynyddoedd Duon (Black Mountains) of the eastern part of the National Park, and which raised up high and sloping back by earth movements is the distinguishing characteristic of the Park. The underlying rock of the Fan, like the Bannau as a whole, are Devonian brown-stones – interbedded red marls, brown sandstones and conglomerates, topped by plateau beds of sandstones and conglomerates which give them a table top appearance. Inevitably their surfaces were covered by great ice-sheets during the Ice Age, valleys like the Wysg (Usk) filled with glaciers moving south-east as far as Môr Hafren (Bristol Channel). As the ice melted moraines – piles of rubbles and silt – were left behind to mark the passing of the glacier. North facing mountains receive little sun, and at their feet the greatest depths of ice form, and pre-existing hollows are further gouged out by ice forming valleys and lakes. Both Llyn y Fan Fach and Llyn y Fan Fawr formed behind moraines. Llyn y Fan Fawr is

Llyn y Fan Fach and the Fan Caerfyrddin

the larger and higher of the two, and close by is the source of the river Tawe which runs down to Swansea, giving the city it's Welsh name of Abertawe, 'estuary of the Tawe'. At the foot of Fan Foel rises the infant river Wysg, on it's way to Casnewydd (Newport). There is a small dam built across Llyn y Fan Fach from where the river Sawdde leaves to enter the river Tywi to the north. There is little marine life in the lakes, though newts have been found in Llyn y Fan Fawr. Llyn y Fan Fach is surrounded by 500 foot/150 metre cliffs, giving it a magical quality in certain light. Fan Hir, the north-eastern face of the Mynydd Du, has at it's foot a three-quarter mile/1.25 kilometre snow scree filled with sandstone blocks which slid there from above.

THE LADY OF THE LAKE AND THE PHYSICIANS OF MYDDFAI

Water has always had a central place in the Celtic belief system. Lakes, rivers and caves were seen as gateways to the gods and to knowledge. They were dangerous places, but places where offerings, whether of metal swords, axes or even bronze cauldrons, could be made in an attempt to appease the gods, or to gain favour and power. Figures of great majesty and mystery were linked with water; after all it was from the lady of another lake that Arthur took the sword and scabbard of Caledfwlch (Excalibur).

To the north-west of Llyn y Fan Fach is the farm of Blaensawdde, the slopes by the lake providing fine grazing for cattle. At some time during the twelfth or thirteenth century the son of the farm, Rhiwallon, was out with the cattle, when he noticed a beautiful girl sitting on the surface of the lake combing her hair, and using the surface of the lake as a mirror. Entranced, and immediately in love, he sought to win her hand by offering his lunch of barley bread. At first she indulged in a little gentle mockery, chanting:

Hard baked is thy bread
It is not easy to catch me,

and to his subsequent and later offer:

Unbaked is thy bread
I will not have thee.

However she must have been a hungry lass for she eventually accepted his offer of part baked bread, and of marriage, bringing with her a dowry of cattle and livestock. They set up home at Esgair-llaethdy, to the east of the village of Myddfai, where she bore him three healthy sons. However she warned him at the time of the marriage that she was one of the Tylwyth Teg, the fairy folk, and that if at any time during their marriage she was struck three times by him she would return back to the lake of Llyn y Fan Fach. Some stories say that only if she was struck by iron would she return to the lake, leading to conjecture that she was a Bronze Age maiden, with no liking for the new iron metal of the Iron Age. Whatever the truth Rhiwallon fell into failure, and after three blows (more taps than blows) she returned home below the surface of the lake, taking with her cattle and oxen. Her family was bereft, her sons roaming the hills in an attempt to find her. Finally she appeared to them, and passed on to them, especially to the eldest, also called Rhiwallon, her knowledge of herbs, of comfort, and of nature's healing powers.

Rhiwallon, the son, duly became personal physician to Rhys Grug, Lord of Dinefwr and Ystrad Tywi, and the ability and wisdom for healing of he and his three sons Cadwgan, Gruffydd and Einion spread out from Wales across Europe. Their home was the village of Myddfai, to the south of Llanymddyfri (Llandovery). Rhys Grug added land and extra benefits to them as token of his esteem. It was he who urged them to commit to writing their vast knowledge of herbs and healing, and their methods of treatment, many surviving in the thirteenth century Llyfr Coch Hergest (Red Book of Hergest), the original manuscripts of which are housed in the British Museum. They had knowledge of some 175 local herbs, many gathered on the slopes of Mynydd Myddfai, to the north of the Wysg reservoir. Over the centuries they and their descendants continued to practice medicine, adding to the written record with new knowledge, with references to astrology, and to classical learning, especially that of Hippocrates. The last of the line of Meddygon Myddfai (the Physicians of Myddfai), a Dr Rice Williams, died in practice in Aberystwyth in 1842. There is a plaque in Myddfai church porch recording many illustrious names.

There has been much recent interest in their work, their holistic approach, their emphasis on patients' responsibilities, and their methods of using just a single herb, or two, three or four only in combination. The National Botanical Gardens at nearby Llanarthne has developed a garden of some of the herbs they used, and have an exhibition of their work. There is even a facsimile reprint available of some of their writings. As an example:

> Whoever is frequently afflicted with a headache let him make a lotion of the vervain, betony, chamomile and red fennel; let him wash his head three times a week therewith and he will be cured.

WALK DIRECTIONS   **[-] denotes Point of Interest**
1. Leave the car park, cross the bridge, and continue for nearly 1.5 miles/2.5 kilometres up along the track to the lake, passing a trout hatchery *en route* – you may see a fine display of trout jumping!
2. Once at the lake bear right uphill on a discernible track and follow it round as it ascends to Bannau Sir Gaer. Continue along the ridge to the cairn and peak of Picws Du. There are good views of the lake, below left, and across to the trig point and

Picws Du

shelter of Fan Brycheiniog.

3. Descend fairly steeply, and at the bottom of the slope choose between continuing on to Fan Foel along the edge of the escarpment, or take a bearing due east on the trig point, and take the short cut.

4. Once at the trig point and shelter on Fan Brycheiniog [1] continue to Bwlch y Giedd some ten minutes away – the path leads off to the left from the track ascending to the unmarked summit of Fan Hir, and descends down to the lake of Llyn y Fan Fawr at an angle of 45°.

5. Once at Llyn y Fan Fawr, go around it, and in preference to choosing a route across the 'flat', pick out a sheep track which keeps to the lower slopes, passing sheep pens *en route*. Continue on back to Llyn y Fan Fach.

6. Once at the lake retrace the track back to the car park.

FACILITIES
None. Youth hostel at Llanddeusant – Cross Inn close by it.

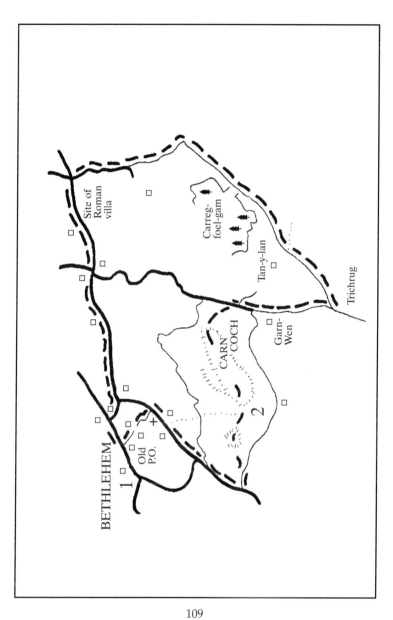

BETHLEHEM

Site of Roman villa

Carreg-foel-gam

Tan-y-lan

Trichrug

Garn-Wen

CARN COCH

Old P.O.

1

2

BETHLEHEM – CARN GOCH – GARN-WEN – CARREG-FOEL-GAM – BETHLEHEM

OS Maps:	1:50 000 Lampeter and Llandovery Landranger 146, Swansea and Gower Landranger 159, Brecon Beacons Landranger 160; Brecon Beacons Western Area Outdoor Leisure 12.
Start:	Bethlehem – also possible to start from Carn Goch where there is a small parking area.
Access:	Bethlehem is on the Bethlehem Road between Llandeilo and Llangadog, on the southern bank of the river Tywi.
Parking:	By the roadside in Bethlehem. There is a small parking area at Carn Goch itself.
Grade:	Moderate – steep sections.

POINTS OF INTEREST:

1. Bethlehem, one of many in Wales, has always offered a rare service in that mail deposited at a special mobile Christmas Post Office has been hand franked and hand dated as Llythyrdy Bethlehem (Bethlehem Post Office). First day covers and seasonal envelopes have been sent out, with special cards and envelopes available on site. Originally the Post Office was closed in 1988; however permission was given for the special mobile to spring into action in the Christmas run-up. The old Post Office has recently been sold; the current Post Office relocating further up the hill on the right.

2. Carn Goch, the red cairn, takes it's name from the bracken that covers the site, and from the old cairn that tops the 700 foot/230 metres high ridge. The ridge is the site of two well preserved Iron Age forts, dating from the late first millenium BC. The smaller of the two – Y Gaer Fach – is to the west,

110

protected by a single drystone rampart. A second wall, different in style, was added at a later date, but was never finished. The entrance was to the east, a narrow passageway of two out-turned ramparts which run down the hillside away from the larger fort above, suggesting the fort was occupied at a different time from it's neighbour. Y Gaer Fawr (the Great Fort) is a much more impressive oval structure protected by it's single massive wall. The outer rampart to the north-west may have been used to herd cattle, however it was never completed. The fort incorporates natural outcrops, and is strongest on it's western side at 6.5 metres high and 25 metres wide. There is evidence for an earlier and larger fort beneath the present one – the prominent cairn, with it's "modern" all-weather shelters, is probably Neolithic or Bronze Age. Eight openings to the fort can, with difficulty, be traced, all with upright slabs; the main entrance may have been to the north-east, with a wide gateway to the south-west. Evidence of round-houses have been found in both forts.

Iron Age forts in the area were normally built on hills of medium height, providing homes, refuges and cattle pounds for the tribes and clans who farmed the land close by. It was a hierarchical society, with, following climate deterioration in the late Bronze Age, a requirement for efficient management of land and farms. Larger Welsh forts, of which Y Gaer Fach is a most impressive example, may have housed anything from 30 to 150 people. While competition for land and resources, and the danger from cattle and slave raiders, meant that defence was an ever present requirement, there was often a 'showing off' element to fort building, more impressive displays of power a kind of style as well as protection. Castell Henllys, near Trefdraeth (Newport) in north Sir Benfro (Pembrokeshire), is a re-creation of an Iron Age hill-fort, complete with round-houses, and gives an insight into Iron Age life.

Carn Goch from the east

WALK DIRECTIONS   **[-] denotes Point of Interest**

1. Starting from Bethlehem walk uphill passed the old Post Office **[1]** to turn shortly right by a walking man sign. Follow the track to buildings, going behind the main building to enter a field by a gate. Keeping to the right-hand edge cross fields to reach a kissing-gate and gate by a chapel and minor road.

2. Turn right onto the minor road. After a short distance, opposite Bronant, there is a path leading left uphill to Carn Goch. Choice to trek up, or to continue half a mile/three-quarters of a kilometre on the minor road to reach the small car park and information panel below Carn Goch.

3. Continue through the hill-forts **[2]** to reach the eastern entrance to Y Gaer Fawr. Continue down to a minor road. The road left will take you down to the minor road between Bethlehem and the A4069. However turn right and continue ahead, ignoring the left turn, to reach the gate giving access to Garn Wen.

4. Just passed the gate take the path to the left, crossing over a stile, and continue to reach a track beyond Garn Wen. Continue uphill on this track, passing ruined farm buildings on the right,

to reach a rectangular enclosure below the ridge of Trichrug, with it's Bronze Age cairn on the skyline.

5. Take the green lane at the top left of the enclosure (heading north-east), ignoring path and stile on the top right. Continue downhill on the lane for well over a mile/1.5 kilometres, ignoring any paths which lead off to right or left, until the path turns sharp left and leads on to join a wider track which itself joins the tarmac road to Carreg-foel-gam farm.

6. Continue on the tarmac road to join the main Bethlehem road to the A4069 – there is to the left the site of a Roman villa, though nothing of it can be seen from the road. Turn left and follow the main road some 1.5 miles/2.5 kilometres back to the starting point, keeping straight on where a sign indicates Carn Goch to the left.

FACILITIES
Bethlehem Post Office currently open
Tuesday 10.00-12.00, Thursday 14.00-16.00 hours.

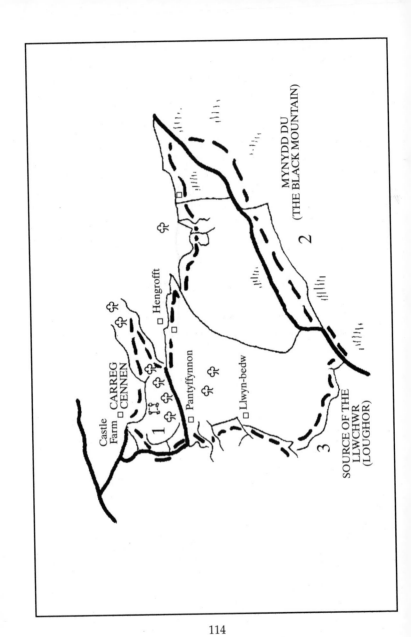

CARREG CENNEN

Castle

Farm

Hengrofft

Pantyffynnon

Llwyn-bedw

MYNYDD DU
(THE BLACK MOUNTAIN)

SOURCE OF THE
LLWCHWR (LOUGHOR)

1

2

3

CARREG CENNEN CASTLE – MYNYDD DU (THE BLACK MOUNTAIN) – LLYGAD LLWCHWR (EYE OF THE LOUGHOR) – CARREG CENNEN CASTLE

OS Maps: 1:50 000 Swansea & Gower Landranger 159; 1:25 000 Brecon Beacons Western Area, Outdoor Leisure 12.

Start: Carreg Cennen castle.

Access: Carreg Cennen castle is to the south-east of Llandeilo, near to the village of Trap.

Parking: Free car park at castle site.

Grade: Moderate.

POINTS OF INTEREST:

1. Stark and majestic on it's sheer limestone crag Carreg Cennen castle dominates the skyline. Like it's near neighbours Dryslwyn and Dinefwr castles on similar rocky crags overlooking the Tywi Valley, this castle was the executive arm of first the Welsh, and then the English domination of the land. The first castle was probably built by the Lord Rhys, Prince of Deheubarth (south-west Wales), in the late twelfth century. His descendant and inheritor Rhys Fychan lost it to the English by the treachery of his mother, before regaining it in 1248. This time he lost it to his uncle, who in turn lost it to Edward I in 1277; the castle then, with rare exceptions, remained in English hands. Ownership was granted to John Giffard, the owner of nearby Llanymddyfri (Llandovery) castle. It was he and his son who, in almost one single period of construction from 1283 to 1321, set about building the present stone castle, in the process obliterating all traces of the previous stronghold.

    The centre of the castle is the compact inner ward, with the gate-house centred on the northern side between two towers. The southern side, overlooking the sheer drop, required only minimal defence. The living quarters and private apartments were set at first floor level adjacent to the eastern wall, above what was probably a storage basement, with the chapel set in it's own tower abutting the wall. The outer ward and barbican belong to the secondary phase of building; the outer ward, on the only level ground, housing the stables, workshops, lime-kilns and smithy. The barbican added an extra measure of defence to the gate house, the rampart consisting of a series of moveable bridges built over pits, and incorporating both right and left turns.

Perhaps the castle's most exciting feature is found in the south-eastern corner of the inner ward, where steps lead down to a vaulted passageway ending in a natural cave. The cave's mouth has been partly walled, and into it set a series of pigeon holes to make a dovecote – pigeons were a much favoured medieval source of meat. There is a small natural reservoir in the cave, but not enough to act as the castle's water supply; two cisterns to the back of the gate house, and a clay lined ditch

Carreg Cennen castle

outside the gate house held this. The cave would have been seen as a defensive weakness, the passageway a defensive device to incorporate the cave within the castle's boundary. The cave has seen earlier human occupancy; four human skeletons and a pendant made from a horse's tooth were found under a layer of stalagmite, dating back to prehistory. It runs back inland as far as the outer ward.

In 1321 the Giffard's made the mistake of choosing the wrong side in the rebellion against Edward II, and ownership of the castle passed through several hands before becoming Crown property in the late fourteenth century. During the Wars of the Roses (1455 to 1487) the castle was garrisoned by the Lancastrian side; there is on the ground floor of the north-western tower an arrow slit remodelled as a musket loop, and, indicating changes in military hardware, may well date from this time. Following the surrender of the castle to the Yorkist forces the castle was demolished in 1462 by five hundred men armed with crowbars and picks. In the late 19th century, in response to the growing number of tourists and visitors (Turner had included a sketch of the castle in his *Dynevor Castle* sketchbook, dating from his fourth tour of Wales in 1798) the then owners, the earls of Cawdor, carried out repairs; the unweathered blue-grey stone dates back to this time. In 1932 it came under the guardianship of the Office of Works, and is now maintained by Cadw.

2. The Mynydd Du (Black Mountain) forms, with Fforest Fawr (the Great Forest), part of the western section of the Bannau Brycheiniog (Brecon Beacons) National Park. It is more desolate and windswept than the central and eastern sections, with fewer towns and people. Stretching from the minor top of Tair Carn Uchaf, just above the mountain road here, a grassy ridge twists across east to Fan Fawr in Fforest Fawr by the A470, at Bannau reservoir, a distance of some 20 miles/32 kilometres. Originally, Fforest Fawr was established by the first Marcher Lord of Aberhonddu (Brecon), Bernard de Neufmarché, half

brother of William I, who by 1091 had occupied Aberhonddu, and by 1110 the Welsh princedom of Brycheiniog. More than just a forest it was a royal hunting reserve comprising forest, grazing land, working farms and mills. To distinguish the Sir Gaerfyrddin (Carmarthenshire) Black Mountain from the Black Mountains in the eastern part of the national park it is often referred to by it's Welsh name of Mynydd Du.

The national park as a whole is predominantly Old Red Sandstone, capped by resistant plateau beds of conglomerates and sandstone which gives it it's distinctive table top appearance. On it's southern edge, noticeably so on Mynydd Du, are scattered rocky outcrops and caves of carboniferous basal grit and limestone. One characteristic of the Carboniferous rocks in the park is the formation of sink, or shake or swallow holes, caused by action of water draining off acid peat onto limestone, draining through cracks in the rock, and by collapse of the basal grit into the underlying caves. Marked on the OS map there are, just to the north of the road, a group of pillow mounds – they have been classified as both a Bronze Age burial site dating from 3000 BC, or else a nineteenth century commercially farmed rabbit warren! The cultivated outer edges of the park give way to grassland, and to moorland, common grazing for sheep and ponies.

3. Llygad Llwchwr, literally the eye of the Llwchwr, is the source for the river Llwchwr which emerges from it's limestone lair to flow south to Rhydaman (Ammanford), and on to form the Burry inlet dividing Sir Gaerfyrddin from the Gŵyr (Gower) peninsula. South from Ammanford it forms the boundary between Sir Gaerfyrddin and west Morgannwg (Glamorgan). Legend has it that the Eye connects, via an underground river, with Llyn y Fan Fach, under Bannau Sir Gaer, though it would take a brave caver to confirm it. A brook from the cave flows into the river Cennen, which itself flows into the river Tywi. The woodland surrounding the castle is a local nature reserve; to the west on the limestone ash predominates, while on the eastern

half oak flourishes on Old Red Sandstone.

WALK DIRECTIONS   **[-] denotes Point of Interest**
1. Starting from the car park follow the path leading up to the castle [1] through the farm of Tir y Castell. Where the castle path leads uphill to the right by the entrance shed, continue ahead through a gate on a downhill path.
2. On reaching the valley floor bear right, ignoring the foot-bridge, and continue on a path keeping the river Cennen to your left. After a short distance cross a stile on the left, descend steps, and continue across stiles to reach a farm road. From here it is easy to see why the castle site was chosen.
3. Bear left across the bridge and continue uphill through Hengrofft farm. Where the track divides, close by a stile on the left, bear right and continue uphill. Turn left onto another track at a junction.
4. Continue on the track to reach a stile giving access to a field. Bear left and continue ahead across fields to shortly gain access to a track leading to the mountain road edging the Mynydd Du [2]. Turn right, and choosing a path through the hillocks to the left follow the line of the road. After crossing a second cattle-grid look for a stile in the stone wall to the right of the road.
5. Cross, and bearing left, shortly cross another stile by two sink-holes. Continue, keeping a wall to your left, and follow a track which bears right and downhill to a gate and stile. To the left is the source of the river Llwchwr [3]. Continue ahead on the track, crossing stiles, to reach a T junction with a better defined track.
6. Bear right – there is a signpost indicating Pantyffynnon – and continue on to Llwyn-bedw. Keep to the left of the buildings and head downhill left to a metal bar stile. Cross, and continuing left across a footbridge, ascend across stiles to reach the minor road by Pantyffynnon.
7. Continue on the road to leave right over a stile, and crossing

a field, aim for the top left to rejoin the starting point.

FACILITIES

Tir y Castell farm has a souvenir shop and tea room; the farm is also a rare breeds trust. They also rent out a torch for exploring the castle cave if you do not have one! Toilets on site at the car park. Pub in nearby Trap.

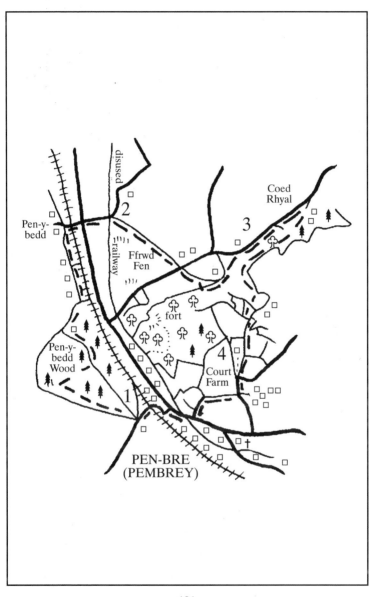

PEN-Y-BEDD WOOD – PEN-Y-BEDD – FFRWD FEN (FFRWD FARM MIRE) – COED – COED RHYAL – PEN-BRE (PEMBREY) – PEN-Y-BEDD WOOD

OS Maps: 1:50 000 Swansea & Gower Landranger 159; 1:25 000 Carmarthen & Kidwelly Explorer 177, Llanelli & Ammanford Explorer 178, Gower Explorer 10.

Start: Forest picnic site.

Access: From Pen-bre follow the road signposted to Pen-bre Country Park. The picnic site is on the right just passed the railway bridge. Pen-bre is on the main bus and train routes from Caerfyrddin (Carmarthen) to Llanelli and Abertawe (Swansea). Pen-bre airfield is close by!

Parking: Car park at picnic site.

Grade: Moderate – woodland and field paths, some road walking.

POINTS OF INTEREST:

1. Pembrey is a corruption of the Welsh name for the village, Pen-bre, meaning 'end of the hill', that is to say at the end of Pen-bre mountain which rises above it. During the Iron Age there were two forts on Pen-bre mountain; the oldest, Carreg Lwyd, was in use from 400BC to 100AD, whilst Court Wood probably continued in occupation until much later – there have been finds of second century Roman pottery on site. Access to the forts is possible from the main road through Pen-bre , Carreg Lwyd the most accessible. The hill may also have been in use during the Bronze Age. Following the Norman conquest of 1066 Pen-bre became part of the Marches of Wales, specifically a manor within the lordship of Cydweli (Kidwelly). The church

was certainly in existence by 1120, however the present building is mostly thirteenth/fourteenth century, and is dedicated to St Illtud. There is in the grounds a memorial to those who have died in shipwrecks on Cefn Sidan sands. One was Adeline Coquelin, niece of Josephine, consort of Napoleon, who perished on *La Jeune Emma* in 1828.

The present coastline, stretching from Pen-bre to Pentywyn (Pendine), is of comparatively recent origin. Most of the dunes have formed since medieval times, many only over the last fifty years. Some 5000/6000 years ago the sea would have been lapping at the foot of Pen-bre mountain. There has been much land reclamation over the centuries, with drainage dykes and sea-wall building continuing from the Middle Ages up until the early nineteenth century. The sands of the silken bank of Cefn Sidan are also of recent origin; it was there in outline only by 1800. 20th century initiatives have been dune stabilisation and the creation of Pen-bre forest. Pen-y-bedd wood, where the walk begins, was formerly a nursery for Pen-bre forest. During the 1930s some thirty local women were employed in growing trees from seed for planting on the already established dunes. The wood is part of Pen-bre forest, and is managed as a Forest Nature Reserve.

Nearby Pen-bre Country Park was itself created as a result of land reclamation in the late 1970s/early 1980s. Formerly the park was the site of a Royal Ordnance factory. At it's peak during the Second World War some 3000 people were employed, production finally ceasing in 1965. The park, one of Wales' top spots, offers a variety of activities, with Cefn Sidan's 8 miles/13 kilometres of sands one of the finest in Europe, with European Blue Flag status. There is still a military presence in the area, with fighter jets attacking aerial targets at the northern end of Pen-bre forest – the targets are attacked from the landward side. One exciting new initiative has been the transformation of the coastal area between Pen-bre and Llanelli from one of industrial dereliction to the Millennium Coastal Park Llanelli, a 14 mile/22 kilometre coastal environmental project. Features, including wetlands, a floating harbour, indoor arena and a watersports centre, are linked by a continuous footpath and cycle-track.

2. A Site of Special Scientific Interest (SSSI), Ffrwd Fen (also known as Ffrwd Farm Mire), is one of the few surviving areas of freshwater marsh in the locality, and is in the care of the Wildlife Trust of South and West Wales. The rare habitats of wet grassland, fen and reed-bed allow specialist species to survive in an area where, in the early 1800s, a large marsh had spread from Cydweli to Pen-bre. One of the now rare species which survive in wetland habitats like Ffrwd Fen is the water-vole, whose lifestyle has recently been the subject of an interpretative land sculpture, mainly for children, at the nearby wetlands reserve of Penclacwydd. There is no access to Ffrwd Fen. The walk follows the north-eastern side of the reserve and accompanies the old Ashburnum canal, abandoned in 1818. For two and a half centuries, from the 1670s to the 1920s, the Ashburnum's were among the leading landowners and industrialists in the area; in 1796 the second Lord Ashburnum began construction on a 1.5 mile/2.5 kilometre long canal reaching from below Coed farm to the Gwendraeth Fawr river at Pill Towyn. To exploit the seams of coal on his land the first Earl had used pack-horses to transport the black gold from nearby Coed Rhyal and Coed y Marchog to ships on the Gwendraeth estuary and the Burry Inlet. The canal, inspired by nearby Kymer's canal at Cydweli, replaced the horses, but by 1818 the coal was virtually exhausted.

A new harbour was built at Pen-bre in 1819 to exploit resources elsewhere in the locality, and to connect the harbour with the Cydweli and Llanelli canal at Pinged marsh a tramroad and the 2 mile/3 kilometre Pen-bre canal had been completed by 1824. The new harbour failed to cope with the level of coal for shipment and in 1832 a new harbour at Burry Port was opened, with an extension to the Cydweli and Llanelli canal completed by 1837. The Cydweli and Llanelli canal was by far the most important in the area. 11 miles/17.5 kilometres long in it's final form, connecting Cydweli, Cwm-mawr and Pont-iets with Burry Port, the canal company was forced by competition from the railways to transform itself by amalgamation with Burry Port Harbour Company in 1866 into the Burry Port and Gwendraeth Valley Railway. The rail lines were built mostly on the canal bed, though occasionally the towpath was used. Like the canal the old railway is disused, though traces of both remain; tracks can be seen embedded in the tarmac road by the entrance to Ffrwd Fen. Burry Port is now the main harbour for Caerfyrddin Bay, with forty boats or more, many occupied, mostly part-time, in fishing for bass or the odd one or two in tangle netting for lobster.

3. Coed Rhyal is, like Ffrwd Fen, managed by the Wildlife Trust

---

THE MEN OF LITTLE HATCHETS

Though only formed since 1800 Cefn Sidan's golden stretch of sands holds hidden secrets of broken timber from the countless number of ships that have foundered here. Names like Smiling Morn, Old Hunter and Prairie Flower recall ships that sought safety in Caerfyrddin Bay, away from the storm ravages of the Môr Hafren (Bristol Channel), only to find themselves aground, or wrecked by the ferocity of the prevailing south westerlies. Crews were lost, and cargo strewn along the tidemark. In the days when authority in the shape of local justices and constables were few in number, and often distant, these spilled cargoes provided a much welcomed addition to local income. Cargo, whether food or materials, that could not find immediate use, could be sold on in local markets in the nearby towns of Llanelli and Caerfyrddin.

It was an attitude that was common to most shore-based communities around the country. Here, in the Pen-bre area, the locals equipped themselves with a locally made tool, a small axe incorporating a claw with which they could cut and rip away sails, ropes, planks and timber on the stranded ship,

---

and break up her cargo. A procession of ponies and carts could be seen hurrying and bustling along the sands after a wreck, often active over two or three days, until all was cleared. Their useful, local tool earned them the title of the Gwŷr y Bwelli Bach (Men of Little Hatchets or the Men of the Small Axes)

Opposition to them came in the form of the local landowners and gentry who owned the shore, and by implication any cargo, and the Crown, who owned the wrecks. J.H. Rees, local Justice of the Peace, took action against the Men of Little Hatchets following the wreck of the *Brother* in December 1833. *En route* from America to Liverpool she and her cargo of four thousand buffalo hides and cotton were wrecked on the sand. Justice Rees reported to the Home Office on the actions of the Men of Little Hatchets.

Carts have been sent from a distance of twenty miles round, to carry away the bales of cotton and timber … the constables … were unable to prevent them from carrying them off, and I was myself assaulted by two men.

How things change.

Cwrt

of South and West Wales. The wood comprises some fourteen acres of sessile oak, much of it coppice re-growth. The wood overlies the coal measures which were exploited by Lord Ashburnum, and there are still open mine-shafts within the woodland; one prominent shaft is fenced off adjacent to the path.
4. Though now ruinous Cwrt farm has a long history. The earliest known family in the Norman manor of Pen-bre were the fourteenth century Butlers of Cwrt farm, and while the present building is not of that period it is the largest surviving Elizabethan building in the county of Caerfyrddin.

WALK DIRECTIONS   **[-] denotes Point of Interest**
1. **[1]** From the car park take the path to the left of the woodland. Continue on the path for half a mile/three quarters of a kilometre to reach a T junction. Turn right onto a wider path and continue to reach a cross-roads. Turn left onto the main forestry track.
2. Continue past the forest office and continue along a permissive path/track to reach the cross-roads at Pen-y-bedd.
3. Turn right, cross the railway line and the main road and go up the minor road. After a short distance cross the old nineteenth century railway line and turn right through a kissing gate onto the path leading Ffrwd Farm Mire nature reserve **[2]**. Signpost here marked Mountain Walks – there are several such signs *en route*, as well as several attractive green stiles!
4. Continue through the reserve to reach a minor road. Cross the road and continue up the track ahead. Do not go all the way to the house, but turn right on a grassy path just before the track bends left. Cross the small open field and enter the wood. There is a signpost 'Llwybr St Illtud.'
5. Turn left. Continue on the woodland path to reach a T junction. Turn left and descend to a minor road. There are good panoramic views ahead, with the flat landscape backed on the left by Pen-bre forest, with directly ahead the Gwendraeth rivers, and perched at the bottom of a ridge Cydweli with it's

Norman castle.

6. Turn right. After a short distance there is a path going up steps on the right into woodland – ignore this, unless you require a short cut through Coed Rhyal!

7. Continue along the road for a quarter of a mile/half a kilometre to join a track bending back right from the road and leading to a property. Cross the metal stile and almost immediately turn right onto a grassy path leading to Coed Rhyal [3]. There is a sign here indicating Mountain Walks.

8. Continue on the woodland path for half a mile/three-quarters of a kilometre to cross a stile into an open field. Turn left and keeping to the left edge continue to the corner of the field where it bends left. Turn right and cross the field to a stile opposite leading into a smaller field.

9. Cross this field, cross another stile and turn and continue right. As you top the rise views open up of the Gŵyr peninsula. Continue along the right edge and descend through field/scrub to reach a road.

10. Continue a short distance on the road until just opposite 'Ar Y Bryn' road turn right onto a path leading past Cwrt's Elizabethan splendour [4].

11. Continue on the path to reach the main A484 through Pen-bre. Turn right, cross the road, and bear left onto the road leading to the Country Park and the starting point.

FACILITIES

All facilities available in Pen-bre and neighbouring Burry Port. Local attractions include Pen-bre Country Park, and the Millennium Coastal Park Llanelli. There is also the Welsh Motor Sports Pembrey Circuit (once a Spitfire airfield) just north of the Country Park offering two and four wheeled entertainment, including truck racing and classic and vintage car races. Near Llanelli at Penclacwydd is the National Wetland Centre of Wales, well worth a visit.

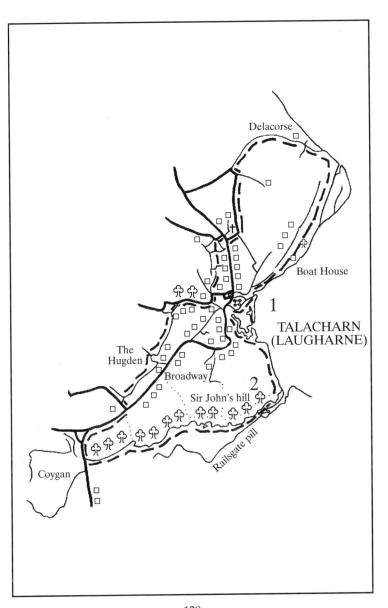

Delacorse

Boat House

1

TALACHARN
(LAUGHARNE)

The
Hugden

Broadway

2

Sir John's hill

Railsgate pill

Coygan

129

TALACHARN (LAUGHARNE) –
SIR JOHN'S HILL – BROADWAY – THE LAQUES
– TALACHARN CHURCH – DELACORSE – THE
BOAT HOUSE – TALACHARN (LAUGHARNE)

OS Maps:	1:50 000 Tenby 158, Swansea & Gower 159: 1:25 000 Carmarthen & Kidwelly Explorer 177.
Start:	Car park below Talacharn Castle. Note: at high tides the foreshore may flood!
Access:	Talacharn is on the A4066 coastal road between Sanclêr (St Clears) and Pentywyn (Pendine). Bus 222 from Caerfyrddin (Carmarthen) to Pentywyn operates daily.
Parking:	Car park below Talacharn castle.
Grade:	Moderate.

POINTS OF INTEREST:

1. Dylan Thomas, the town's most famous resident, described Talacharn as 'this timeless, mild, beguiling island of a town … there is nowhere like it anywhere at all'. Talacharn has always been proud of it's independence, and it has the history to prove it. It was the successive male members of the de Brian family – conveniently, and as if to prove a point, all called Guy – who remodelled and strengthened the existing Norman castle from the late twelfth to the late fourteenth centuries, and it was in 1291 that the town was granted it's charter, still in force. One of the burgesses' entitlements is shares in land at the Hugden, one of the very rare survivals of medieval strip fields in Britain – the walk passes along the foot of the Hugden; the strips well preserved. Little now remains of the medieval town, though the original defence lines and the position of the town gates are roughly known. The name Laugharne derives from the Welsh

Talacharn, the old name predating the thirteenth century charter, and this in itself appears to be a corruption of Tal la Corran, the headland of the Corran, the river which flows through the town to meet the river Taf below the castle. This once tidal inlet has now been paved over to form the Grist – the name probably derives from a grist mill that one stood here – the centre of the Grist is marked by the Celtic cross. The salt-marsh and creeks which lean out seawards have formed recently, over the last hundred years or so.

The castle itself has a mellow, attractive look and feel; built of local Old Red Sandstone with additions of attractive green stone by Guy de Brian VII in the mid fourteenth century Dylan Thomas found it in Poem in October – 'as brown as owls'. After the death of Guy de Brian VII in 1390 the castle's fortunes declined, only to be revived in the late sixteenth century when it was granted by Elizabeth I to Sir John Perrot. With defence less a priority in Elizabethan times Perrot set about transforming the castle, as he did with his main residence at Carew (Caeriw) in Sir Benfro (Pembrokeshire), into a luxurious Elizabethan mansion. With Perrot's arrest for treason the castle's fortunes once again declined. In the late nineteenth century, with the castle a Romantic ruin, the outer ward was laid out in a formal garden, and these, together with the castle, have been restored and are open during the summer months. Both Thomas and Richard Hughes, author of *A High Wind in Jamaica*, have found the castle's gazebo conducive to writing. Talacharn's church, dedicated to St Martin, dates from the late fourteenth century, with it's two porches and the majority of it's windows dating from the late nineteenth century. There is a fine disk headed ninth/tenth century sculptured cross, now kept in the church for safe-keeping. Dylan and Caitlin Thomas are buried in the churchyard, their graves marked by a simple white cross. There is a memorial plaque to Dylan Thomas in the church, a replica of the one at Poet's Corner at Westminster Abbey. Thomas first moved to Talacharn in May 1938, leaving for

Talacharn castle

London in July 1940. He returned again in March 1949 when the town and the Boat House became his main home. The Boat House and the writing shed (Talacharn's first garage!) are now a heritage centre. Thomas' last major work, *Under Milk Wood*, was mostly written in Talacharn, (and often about Talacharn), and was first performed in the USA, some six months before his death.

2. Sir John's hill turns it's back on Talacharn to look out over the rivers Taf and Tywi and over Talacharn and Pentywyn Burrows, western Wales' largest spit and sand dune system. The system itself is recent, having begun to develop only since 1800. Prior to this the coastline would have been marked by the present low line of hills, with the river Taf much wider. The coastline is now stable, and has been much used as marginal grazing land. That area not now used as a firing range by the Ministry of Defence, who have had access to the area since the trial Normandy

landings took place here, is under the care of Carmarthenshire County Council (Cyngor Sir Caerfyrddin). At the edge of Sir John's hill, and now demolished by quarrying, Coygan cave once stood, slung like a hunchback and looking out over a once cool and grassy plain that in prehistoric times was Caerfyrddin Bay. There would have been stands of birch and pine, with herds of mammoth, bison and reindeer. Before it's extinction the cave was excavated five times, the last in 1963. Most of the bones found were woolly rhinoceros, cave bear, Irish elk, bison, reindeer and hyena, and was most probably home to that master scavenger, the hyena. Stone tools found indicate human occupation at some stage by Neanderthal man, and have been dated to 45,000 years bp (before present). Later Neolithic, and possibly, Mesolithic peoples found the site conducive to more permanent settlement. From the late eighteenth century until the early twentieth the limestone quarried at Coygan was transported along a horse drawn tramway to waiting ships at Railsgate pill – lime was required as fertilizer and mortar; transport is now by road. On his return to Talacharn to live in 1949 Dylan Thomas wrote Over Sir John's Hill in celebration

… and a black cap of jackdaws Sir John's just hill dons, and again the gulled birds hare to the hawk on fire, the halter height, over Towy's fins …

WALK DIRECTIONS   **[-] denotes Point of Interest**
1. Starting from the car park walk along the foreshore away from Talacharn [1] along the metal track towards the pumping station. Note: this section can flood at high tides.
2. Just before the station and a bench take the waymarked path on the right leading up into woods and on to Sir John's hill.
3. Just over half a mile/three-quarters of a kilometre, and by a viewpoint/notice board, there is a choice of two paths. Take the left path and descend, passing another notice board, until the path levels [2].

4. Continue on the path, passing in front of Salt House farm and kennels (basset hounds), and continue on to reach the minor road and the quarry at Coygan.

5. Turn right, and again right at a 'No Through Road', to meet the main road. Continue ahead to reach Broadway Caravan and Camping Park. At the park take the minor road left, signposted Llansadurnon.

6. Almost immediately, opposite the entrance to the park, leave the minor road and cross a waymarked stile right, indicated by a walking man sign, and follow the path across the field – note the layout of the old strip fields of the Hugden.

7. Where the field path meets a hedge adjacent to houses bear left, keping the hedge on your right, and shortly, at the corner of the hedge, take the clearly defined path on the right leading off between trees.

8. Continue on the path, crossing a stone foot-bridge, and passing close by a house on the right, join the track leading down to a minor road. Turn right.

9. Continue and take the next minor road on the left, opposite an old water pump and a sign for The Laques.

10. Continue ahead and take Holloway Road, which leads off ahead between houses.

11. Shortly join a path, and then cross two fields to meet a minor road – Horsepool Road. Turn right and at the main road cross to the church.

12. Walk passed the church and take the road immediately left, initially cobbled, marked 'Unsuitable for Wide Vehicles'. Continue ahead, uphill and then left. It is possible to join this road directly from the churchyard if preferred.

13. Continue to meet a T junction. Turn right and continue downhill to Delacorse and the river. Continue across fields to join a woodland path.

14. Continue on the path, cross the road leading down to the shore, and continue directly ahead, passing Dylan Thomas' Boat House and his writing shed.

15. Just passed the shed, and opposite a whitewashed building and by the sign for the Boat House, turn left down steps to reach the paved walkway leading below the castle and returning you to the starting point.

Thomas' writing shed

FACILITIES
Most available in Talacharn. Home from home for Dylan Thomas fans!